# The Character of the Kingdom

**CHALLENGE**
**BIBLE STUDY GUIDES**

Old Testament Women by Sara Buswell
  *Believers or Beguilers*
  *Courageous Overcomers*
  *Vain or Visionary*
  *Selfless or Selfish*

When God Calls by Sara Buswell
  *Responding to God's Call*
  *Submitting to God's Call*

The Life of David by Mary Nelle Schaap
  *Seeing God in the Life of Young David*
  *Seeing God in the Life of David the King*

The Parables of Jesus by Ward B. Schaap
  *The Character of the Kingdom*
  *The Character of the King*

Portraits of Jesus from the Gospel Writers by Mary Nelle Schaap
  *Portraits of Jesus from Matthew and Mark*
  *Portraits of Jesus from Luke and John*

Studies in Old Testament Poetry by Kathleen Buswell Nielson
  *This God We Worship*
  *Resting Secure*

# The Character of the Kingdom

## Studies in the Parables

*Ward B. Schaap*

**Baker Books**

A Division of Baker Book House Co
Grand Rapids, Michigan 49516

© 1994 by Ward B. Schaap
Published by Baker Books
a division of Baker Book House Company
P.O. Box 6287, Grand Rapids, MI 49516–6287

ISBN 0–8010–8370–2

Printed in the United States of America

I wish to dedicate these study guides to my wife, Mary Nelle, without whose inspiration, encouragement, and considerable help this project would never have been completed.

# Study Plan

1. Read the questions at the beginning of each lesson.

2. Read the Scripture passage(s) listed and be aware of the questions as you read. Allow time to think about words or phrases or incidents that are especially meaningful to you. Underline them in your Bible.

3. Formulate initial answer(s) to questions.

4. If possible, discuss answers with a friend or group.

5. Read the lesson commentary.

6. Revise answers, if necessary.

7. Apply your answers to your life as God directs.

# Contents

# Foreword

*P*reparing these studies on Jesus' parables has been thoroughly enjoyable—pure pleasure! I first became involved with them when I volunteered to lead an adult Sunday school class in a study of this topic in the year following my retirement from the faculty of Indiana University. For the first time in my life, I felt as though I had ample time to read, research, and study as I prepared the weekly lessons. As the term progressed, I became more and more fascinated by the parables and found that Jesus used them to present almost every facet of the gospel message. I became aware that Jesus used these amazing stories for more than illustrations of the spiritual points he was making; often they alone were his point and were given without further explanation.

Our goal in these studies is to understand Jesus' parables in their original time and setting—to try to put ourselves on the scene so that we will be instructed, prodded, challenged, and changed as were those who heard these stories directly from Jesus. I know that I am not the same person I was when I began these studies, and I doubt that anyone who works through them carefully can escape being affected in a major way.

As a teacher in a university, I discovered quickly that the students who learned the most were those who studied and dug things out for themselves and didn't just come to class and listen to lectures. I saw this in my Sunday school class as well. The most valuable aspect of this study is working through the questions at the beginning of each chapter and formulating your own answers. What you read in a book on the parables you may soon forget, but what you dig out of the Bible and think through on your own you will remember and incorporate into your life.

While reading commentaries and published works on the parables, I became aware of the striking changes that have occurred over the centuries in the way Jesus' parables have been interpreted. The early and medieval church fathers treated them as allegories in which every facet and detail had a spiritual meaning that required interpretation. Some of these interpretations were quite fanciful and could not possibly have been what Jesus wanted to convey to his first-century A.D. audience. For example, in the parable of the prodigal son, the ring the father gave to his lost son upon his return home was said to represent Christian baptism, and the feast given by the father in honor of his son was associated with the Lord's Supper, even though these concepts would have been completely unknown to Jesus' audience.

Beginning about the turn of this century the pendulum swung far in the other direction. Biblical scholars reacted against this overly allegorical approach and decided that the parables characteristic of Jesus were short oral stories which, to be understood by his listeners, were intended to have only one main point. This view, which in the intervening years has become widely accepted, has been challenged more recently by some conservative scholars who believe that the distinction between allegory and parable cannot be sharply drawn and who see no need to assume that Jesus' longer parables, such as "The Prodigal Son," "The Good Samaritan," and "The Sower," had only one point when originally told. They argue that many of the parables make more than one spiritual point very naturally and that these points are entirely consistent with the structure of the story and would be easily remembered by Jesus' listeners. For example, in "The Prodigal Son" there is important spiritual truth related to the actions of each of the three main characters, and one would be hard pressed to select the one single lesson of the story. (For those interested in these textual matters, the recent book by Craig Blomberg, *Interpreting the Parables,* presents a summary from an evangelical perspective.)

This intermediate approach, which represents a partial return of the pendulum, will be followed in this study. We will assume that the present-day translations of the Bible accurately present Jesus' words, and we will not restrict ourselves to finding only one main point in each parable. We will look for all the important spiritual lessons by examining each story in a straightforward, natural way, seeking to be consistent with its context, structure, and characters. In doing this, we will attempt to avoid over-allegorizing by limiting ourselves to interpretations that are consistent with the main point associated with each principal character or feature of the narrative.

Of the thirty to forty parables told by Jesus, I have selected nineteen of the better-known ones for inclusion in these studies. Twelve of these are treated in this volume, of which six are covered in chapter 4. Another seven are the subject of the second volume. Somewhat arbitrarily, I have divided the parables between the two volumes according to chronology, i.e., the early and the later parables. The early parables are concerned chiefly with the characteristics of the kingdom of heaven Jesus was announcing. This was a kingdom that was new and different ("Patch and Wineskins"), a kingdom whose message would receive mixed response ("Sower"), a kingdom of mixed character ("Wheat and Weeds," "Dragnet"), of great value ("Treasure," "Pearl"), of certain growth ("Mustard Seed," "Leaven"), a kingdom whose citizenship is gained by repentance and faith ("Two Debtors") and one which sets high standards for its citizens ("Good Samaritan," "Rich Fool").

Jesus' later parables, the subject of the companion volume, deal mainly with the character of the King himself. He is presented as one who hears the petitions of those in need ("Friend at Midnight," "Persistent Widow"), one who is patient and loving ("Prodigal Son"), one who is both sovereign and just ("Rich Man and Lazarus," "Workers in the Vineyard," "Royal Wedding Banquet"), and one who rewards his faithful servants who await his return ("Talents").

It is my hope and prayer that you will enjoy and profit from these studies as much as I have. Jesus' parables are very practical, and reflecting on these teachings has forced me to examine my own attitudes and life and to make changes. Even more importantly, I have come to know, appreciate, and worship in a deeper way than ever before the Teacher himself, who is greater than his teachings, for as a famous preacher once said, "Jesus came not so much to present the gospel, but that there might be a gospel to present."

### Suggestions for Further Reading and Study

I wish to recognize and cite a number of books and commentaries that were particularly helpful to me as I prepared these studies on the parables. Anyone wishing to do further reading or research on the parables would do well to begin with these sources.

Among the commentaries on Matthew and/or Luke consulted, those by William Barclay (Westminster Press), D. A. Carson (Zondervan), William Hendriksen (Baker), and I. H. Marshall (Paternoster) proved to be especially valuable. Of the many books written on the parables, the two volumes by Kenneth Bailey, *Poet and Peasant* and *Through Peasant Eyes* (Eerdmans) in particular, and the volume by Joachim Jeremias, *The Parables of Jesus* (Westminster), provide much valuable insight into Middle Eastern customs as well as textual matters. The critical study by Craig Blomberg, *Interpreting the Parables* (Intervarsity Press), and the book by David Wenham, *The Parables of Jesus* (IVP), both give interpretations of all the parables as well as summaries of the history of their interpretation. Practical applications of the parables are stressed in the interesting volumes by Lloyd Ogilvie, *Autobiography of God* (Regal Books), and by Helmut Thielicke, *The Waiting Father* (Harper). The books by William Coleman, *The Pharisees' Guide to Total Holiness* (Bethany House), by Paul Johnson, *A History of the Jews* (Harper and Row), and by Joachim Jeremias, *Jerusalem in the Time of Jesus* (Fortress Press), provide valuable historical information on the Pharisees and the Jewish nation at the time of Christ. Finally, an excellent summary article on the parables is included in Walter Elwell's *Encyclopedia of the Bible* (Baker).

## The Parables of Jesus

| | Luke | Matthew | Mark |
|---|---|---|---|
| New cloth on old coat | 5:36 | 9:16 | 2:21 |
| New wine in used wineskins | 5:37–38 | 9:17 | 2:22 |
| Houses on rock and on sand | 6:47–49 | 7:24–27 | |
| The moneylender | 7:41–43 | | |
| Sower and soils | 8:5–8 | 13:3–8 | 4:3–8 |
| Lamp under a bowl | 8:16; 11:33 | 5:14–15 | 4:21–22 |
| The Good Samaritan | 10:30–37 | | |
| Friend in need | 11:5–8 | | |
| Rich fool | 12:16–21 | | |
| Watchful servants | 12:35–40 | | |
| Faithful servant | 12:42–48 | 24:45–51 | |
| Unfruitful fig tree | 13:6–9 | | |
| Mustard seed | 13:18–19 | 13:31–32 | 4:30–32 |
| Yeast | 13:20–21 | 13:33 | |
| Best places at a wedding banquet | 14:7–14 | | |
| Great banquet and reluctant guests | 14:16–24 | | |
| Cost of being a disciple | 14:28–33 | | |
| Lost sheep | 15:4–6 | 18:12–13 | |
| Lost coin | 15:8–10 | | |
| Lost son | 15:11–32 | | |
| Shrewd manager | 16:1–8 | | |
| Rich man and Lazarus | 16:19–31 | | |
| Master and servant | 17:7–10 | | |
| Persistent widow | 18:2–5 | | |
| Pharisee and tax collector | 18:10–14 | | |
| Pounds | 19:12–27 | | |
| Tenants | 20:9–16 | 21:33–41 | 12:1–9 |
| Fig tree | 21:29–32 | 24:32–33 | 13:28–29 |
| Weeds | | 13:24–30 | |
| Hidden treasure | | 13:44 | |
| Pearl | | 13:45–46 | |
| Net | | 13:47–48 | |
| Unmerciful servant | | 18:23–34 | |
| Workers in the vineyard | | 20:1–16 | |
| Two sons | | 21:28–31 | |
| Wedding banquet and garment | | 22:2–14 | |
| Ten virgins | | 25:1–13 | |
| Talents | | 25:14–30 | |
| Sheep and goats | | 25:31–36 | |
| Growing seed | | | 4:26–29 |

From *Baker Encyclopedia of the Bible*, Walter A. Elwell, ed. (Grand Rapids: Baker Books, 1988), 1612. Used with permission.

# 1

## Jesus, the Master Teacher

| Primary Scripture Reading | Supplementary References |
|---|---|
| Matthew 5, 6, 7 | Matthew 12:9–14; 20:29–34 |
| Mark 1:14–2:17 | Mark 1:40–42; 10:13–16 |
| | Luke 7:11–15; 10:25–37 |
| | Hebrews 4:12 |

### Questions for Study and Discussion

1. Think back to teachers you have had who made you want to study and learn. What made them effective?

   List what you think are the characteristics of a good teacher.

2. Read Mark 1:14 through 2:17, imagining that you've never heard anything about Jesus before. Discipline yourself to observe only what is given in the text. In each paragraph or scene, notice the people whose lives Jesus touched, his attitude and actions toward them, and their reaction to him. On a sheet of paper tabulate your observations under the following headings:

| Verse | People Affected | Jesus' Attitude | Jesus' Action | People's Reaction |
|---|---|---|---|---|
| | | | | |
| | | | | |
| | | | | |
| | | | | |

3. If you had been in the audience in the episode in Mark 2:1–12, how would you have answered the "which is easier" question?

   What dilemma did this question pose for the Pharisees?

4. Why do you think Jesus' miracles did not have a positive effect on the Pharisees' attitude toward him?

   When Jesus said, "I have not come to call the righteous, but sinners" (Mark 2:17), what do you suppose he meant?

5. Read Matthew 5:21–48 and notice the authority with which Jesus taught. Scan Matthew 6:19 to 7:29 and jot down ten examples of figures of speech or illustrations drawn from everyday life that Jesus used to make his points.

   Which ones of these are particularly meaningful to you, and why?

6. For each of the following incidents, imagine what your reaction to Jesus as a person would have been if you had been present:
   Matthew 20:29–34

   Mark 1:40–42

   Mark 10:13–16

   Luke 7:11–15

   In your own words explain what compassion means to you, and give an example of it from your own experience.

7. Scan the titles of Jesus' parables at the front of this study guide. Recalling as many of the stories as you can, which of them in your opinion illustrate particularly well the truth of the last phrase of Hebrews 4:12?

Why?

It is the teacher's mission . . . by sympathy, by example, and by every means of influence—by objects for the senses, by facts for the intelligence—to excite the minds of pupils, to stimulate their thoughts

John Milton Gregory
*The Seven Laws of Teaching*

Two of my high school teachers stand out in my memory above all others. They were as different as night and day, yet each was effective in a special way. I can still picture Mr. Spores as he lectured on American history or civics. There were times when his lectures were a little boring, but what impressed us was that he intensely cared that we learn what he was teaching. We could sense his genuine anxiety if we were restless and inattentive. His attitude and concern for us made us want to listen. Miss Mentink, on the other hand, was lively and innovative. She kept us on our toes because we never knew what to expect in her English classes. She peppered us with questions about our assignments and seemed to make it her personal mission to teach us to understand and appreciate poetry. I can still hear her intonations and dramatic expression as she read us poems such as "The Bells," "Congo," and "Chicago." She made stories and poems come alive for us, and that's undoubtedly why I can still remember some of them decades later.

The teacher who influenced and changed more lives than any other person who ever lived was Jesus of Nazareth. By any standard, he was a master communicator. He knew how to reach people where they were and lead them to new thoughts and understanding. The impact of his person and his teaching is incalculable. He and his message literally changed the course of history. And yet we have no record of anything he wrote; we have only his words as they were remembered and collected from his stories and discourses. What he said was etched on the minds of his listeners and never forgotten.

Jesus began his ministry quietly. He first gathered about him a band of twelve close followers, but his teaching began to attract larger and larger crowds. Friends told friends and neighbors told neighbors, "You've never heard a teacher like this. He's different! What he says makes sense." Some of the people's reactions to Jesus recorded in the Gospels are these: "The people were all so amazed that they asked each other, 'What is this? A new teaching—and with authority!'" (Mark 1:27). "The large crowd listened to him with delight" (Mark 12:37). "He taught in their synagogues, and everyone praised him" (Luke 4:15). "No one ever spoke the way this man does" (John 7:46). "The crowds were amazed at his teaching, because he taught as one who had authority, and not as their teachers of the law" (Matt. 7:28–29).

How could the teaching of this carpenter's son who had no regular rabbinical training have such an impact on people? What did he say that was so arresting and compelling? How did he say it? What made him such an effective communicator? These are questions we will explore throughout these studies. In this initial chapter we will take an overall look at the way Jesus taught and examine the characteristics of his approach to teaching.

## Characteristics of Jesus' Teaching

### Jesus Taught with Compassion

When Jesus taught, he wasn't just dispensing dry information. He put his heart and soul into what he said, and the people recognized this. They sensed his sincere love and concern for them as individuals, regardless of their social status, reputation, or nationality. The crowds that followed Jesus observed him at close range for hours at a time. With no public address systems, they had to crowd in around him to be able to hear him. With this constant close scrutiny, if there had been any insincerity, hypocrisy, impatience, or lack of concern, it would have been detected immediately, and Jesus' message would have lost its effectiveness. Instead, those nearest him saw a level of love and compassion that amazed and attracted them.

Jesus was under such constant pressure from the crowds that it worried the disciples and made them want to protect him, even from mothers who wanted him to bless their children (Mark 10:13–16). But Jesus never allowed his tiredness to be used as an excuse to turn people away. On one occasion, after Jesus had been so busy teaching crowds of people that he and the disciples didn't even have time to eat, Jesus made plans to slip away with his disciples to a quiet place to rest. But when they got there, they found that the crowds had followed them. What was Jesus' reaction? Mark tells it best:

> Then, because so many people were coming and going that they did not even have a chance to eat, [Jesus] said to them,

"Come with me by yourselves to a quiet place and get some rest." So they went away by themselves in a boat to a solitary place. But many who saw them leaving recognized them and ran on foot from all the towns and got there ahead of them. When Jesus landed and saw a large crowd, he had compassion on them, because they were like sheep without a shepherd. So he began teaching them many things (Mark 6:31–34).

Jesus' reactions to people constantly astonished the disciples. When a leper called out to him begging to be healed, Jesus reached out and actually touched the leper and healed him. We can only imagine the disciples' thoughts as they watched Jesus touch this afflicted outcast whom everyone else avoided. And what about the leper's thoughts and feelings as he was touched by another human being, perhaps for the first time in years? Through his compassionate actions and attitudes, Jesus was teaching at a depth far greater than words alone could penetrate.

### Jesus Taught Inductively

When Jesus taught, he did not start with a stated proposition, principle, or doctrine and then deduce practical lessons and applications from it, as is common in sermons we hear today. Instead, he usually taught by using a series of stories or examples drawn from everyday life and experiences to reveal to his audience the basic spiritual truth he wanted to convey. Jesus' Sermon on the Mount in Matthew 5, 6, and 7 is an outstanding example of this type of teaching. In this sermon he defined true righteousness by means of an unforgettable sequence of stories and illustrations. He gave his audience one example after another with no apparent climax, and yet each one presented a different facet of what obedience to God's law really meant. More often than not, Jesus left his stories unexplained. He trusted his listeners to remember them and ponder them and then to accept the truth once they understood it. In this way Jesus' listeners were led to discover for themselves the truths about God, his kingdom, and what obedience to God really meant in their lives. This made listening and learning exciting, personal, and unforgettable.

### Jesus Asked Probing Questions

Those listening to Jesus could not just sit back, enjoy his stories, and remain detached. Often his stories ended with penetrating questions which they could not duck. When an expert in the law asked Jesus, "And who is my neighbor?" Jesus replied with the parable of the good Samaritan (Luke 10). However, at the end of the story, Jesus confronted the scribe with a question of his own: "Which of these three do you think was a neighbor to the man who fell into the hands of robbers?"

Three examples of Jesus' use of questions are found in Matthew 21 where Jesus was confronted by his opposition. In the first (vv. 23–27), he parried a question from the chief priests and elders with one of his own, which stopped them cold and which they refused to answer. In the other two (vv. 28–46), he told them parables, and ended each with a question to them which put them in a difficult spot. The religious leaders were forced to understand and face the point Jesus was making about them, and it made them angry.

### Jesus Taught with Authority

What amazed people about Jesus' teaching was his boldness and his obvious confidence and authority. The scribes, who had the responsibility of teaching and interpreting biblical laws, lacked this (Matt 7:28–29). When the scribes taught the Scriptures in the synagogue, they would review the interpretations and judgments of previous commentators. They hesitated to give any conclusions or opinions of their own unless they were supported by some esteemed prior authority. Jesus, on the other hand, ignored many of the oral traditions, both in his teaching and his actions, and cut through the mass of accumulated rules and regulations to bring his hearers face to face with the true thrust and intent of God's commandments. In Matthew 5 we have a clear picture of Jesus' authoritative teaching, for six times in the last half of this chapter Jesus says, "You have heard that it was said . . . but I tell you." Each time he contrasts the letter of the law with a higher standard that meets the essence of the commandment. Is it any wonder that the crowds were amazed at the authority of his words, and also that he evoked the hatred and opposition of many of the religious leaders?

### Jesus Used Stories and Figures of Speech

Jesus' teaching was colorful and exciting, sprinkled with narratives and picturesque speech patterns which he used to make spiritual truth easier to visualize and grasp. He chose casual incidents and familiar objects, often things he saw at the very moment, to illustrate abstract concepts. His teaching caught the attention of his listeners, penetrated their minds, and stirred their hearts. God's care of the birds and flowers was used to teach them not to worry (Matt. 6:25–34). The story of the prodigal son dramatized God's love and forgiveness (Luke 15:11–32). The illustration of a shepherd searching for his lost sheep and carrying it home on his shoulders made God's love infinitely more real to his audience than just a plain statement of that fact that God loved them (Luke 15:1–7).

Jesus made extensive use of similes to illustrate in a visual way the points he was making. A simile is a figure of speech that makes a comparison of two unlike objects, connecting them with words such as *like, so,* or *as.* Many of Jesus' parables begin with similes, which are then extended and incorporated into longer narratives. Several such examples are found in Matthew 13, where Jesus discussed the kingdom of heaven, a subject he very much wanted his listeners to understand: "The kingdom of heaven is like a mustard seed. . . . The kingdom of heaven is like yeast. . . . The kingdom of heaven is like treasure hidden in a field," and so on.

Jesus also used metaphors, which, like similes, compare one object to another by substitution but do not employ connecting words such as *like* or *as*. Jesus used a striking series of metaphors to make his remarkable "I am" claims in John's Gospel: "I am the bread of life," "I am the light of the world," "I am the gate," "I am the good shepherd," "I am the resurrection and the life." These simple metaphors enhance and broaden our understanding of the Lord in a beautiful way. Metaphors are generally stronger and deeper comparisons than similes. For example, Jesus' statement, "I am the bread of life," is a much stronger and more meaningful description of himself than the statement, "I am like the bread of life." Similarly, the metaphor, "I am the door," says a lot more about Jesus than would the simile, "I am like a door."[1]

Perhaps the most distinctive and interesting characteristic of Jesus' teaching was his extensive use of parables to make the points he wished to convey. About thirty to forty are recorded in the Gospels, the exact number depending on the definition used. Surprisingly, they comprise more than a third of Jesus' recorded words.

The word *parable* comes from the Greek verb *paraballo*, meaning "to place side by side" or "to compare." Many of us will remember the definition of a parable we learned in Sunday school: an earthly story with a heavenly meaning. This is a more precise definition: a short story told for the

---

[1]The term *metaphor* can also be used in a broader sense for any figure of speech or narrative form in which one thing represents or stands for something else which is fundamentally different. In this broader sense, similes, parables, and allegories can all be referred to as metaphorical.

purpose of presenting moral or religious truth by means of comparisons with natural or ordinary things or events.[2]

Allegories also use fictional stories or events to illustrate moral principles. The principal difference between parables and allegories is that allegories are generally much longer, have more characters and events, and all details of the story are intended to have a symbolic meaning. John Bunyan's *Pilgrim's Progress* is a classic example of an allegory. On the other hand, Jesus' parables, always given orally, should not be considered allegories, since they are usually very short and apparently are intended to make only a few major points.

Another speech pattern skillfully employed by Jesus was the paradox. These expressions seem on the surface to be self-contradictory or absurd, but at a deeper level express fundamental truth. Jesus used them to shock his audiences and awaken them to understand that the value system of the kingdom of heaven is opposite to that of this world. Because of their reverse twist, paradoxes are especially striking and easily remembered. Following are examples of paradoxes:

So the last will be first, and the first will be last (Matt. 20:16).

For whoever wants to save his life will lose it, but whoever loses his life for me and for the gospel will save it (Mark 8:35).

The greatest among you will be your servant. For whoever exalts himself will be humbled, and whoever humbles himself will be exalted (Matt. 23:11–12).

[2]This is the commonly accepted meaning. Actually, the Greek noun *parabole* is used more broadly in the Gospels. It is used also to describe shorter figures of speech such as similes and proverbial sayings, including the proverb, "Physician, heal yourself!" in Luke 4:23.

## The Purpose of the Parables

Was Jesus wasting time telling many stories when he had such an important message to deliver and so little time to do it? Why did he rely heavily on parables, especially toward the end of his ministry? Jesus understood the human mind and the learning process. He knew that spiritual truth is grasped best when it is given in the form of illustrations or narratives drawn directly from the listeners' life experiences. He was a master at leading people from the concrete to the abstract. It is difficult to define love, mercy, kindness, pride, and self-righteousness, but Jesus made these concepts come alive through his examples and stories. And yet this evidently wasn't the whole answer to his use of parables. As Jesus' opposition from the religious leaders grew and hardened, he began to teach more and more through parables. When the disciples asked about this trend, Jesus gave a puzzling reply.

> The disciples came to him and asked, "Why do you speak to the people in parables?" He replied, "The knowledge of the secrets of the kingdom of heaven has been given to you, but not to them. Whoever has will be given more, and he will have an abundance. Whoever does not have, even what he has will be taken from him. This is why I speak to them in parables: 'Though seeing they do not see; though hearing, they do not hear or understand'" (Matt. 13:10–13).

Jesus' answer must have surprised the disciples as much as it does us. Apparently, parables can both reveal and conceal truth. But how can this be? Perhaps it is because parables make their points indirectly. Parables consist of stories in which the hearers are invited to compare, evaluate, and pass judgment on the main characters and their actions. In doing this, the hearers have the opportunity and implicit challenge to apply this evaluation and judgment to themselves, which they may not choose to do. A prime example of this is found in the life of King David after his sin with Bathsheba. Nathan the prophet confronted David by telling him a parable (2 Sam. 12:1–14). David understood the story itself and reacted to it by condemning the hard-hearted rich man who took the poor man's pet lamb; yet he did not apply the truth of the story to himself and his own sin until Nathan pointed his finger at him and said, "You are the man!"

Jesus' parables always throw out the challenge: "You are the man!" Some of his parables present positive examples of the righteousness required of those who are God's children and members of his kingdom, while others depict negative images of injustice or self-righteousness. In either case, we have the opportunity to put ourselves into the story and apply the truth of the parable to our own lives. If we listen with open minds and receptive spirits, we will gain fresh insight into our spiritual condition; if we are self-righteous and unreceptive, we will not see or admit that the story applies to us. The challenges of the parables are as important for us today as they were to Jesus' audiences two thousand years ago.

### Understanding the Parables

Our desire in these studies is to dig into the parables and to understand their meaning so that we are challenged by the truths Jesus intended to teach. To do this, we will seek answers to questions such as those discussed below.

### 1. What Is the Context of the Parable

What was Jesus' main concern when he told a particular parable, and what question or problem was he addressing? To whom was he speaking and why? If the passage does not answer these questions explicitly, then we must try to discover why the Gospel writer placed the parable where he did in his book. What did he think the parable meant? We will assume that the Gospel writers, as close as they were to the time and place the parable was given, had a good understanding of its meaning in its original situation, and therefore included it at an appropriate place in their texts.

### 2. What Is the Literal Meaning of the Story

We will examine the narrative for its main characters, their actions, choices and responses, and try to see the picture the story conveyed to its first-century A.D. Jewish audience. For example, the parable of the friend at midnight (Luke 11:5–8) takes on new meaning when we understand the crucial role of bread in the meals of that day. The structure of each story—its climax, repetition of key words or thoughts, and any unusual reversals or surprising turns of events—also provides clues to its meaning. Understanding the significance of the story in its original context increases our chances of grasping what Jesus intended to teach.

### 3. What Is the Spiritual or Metaphorical Meaning of the Parable

Whom or what do the main characters represent, other than themselves, and what are the religious implications of their actions or reactions? Our interpretations should be those that would make sense to Jesus' audience with their particular religious background and economic and cultural situation. It is important to be aware of Old Testament concepts and religious practices. Nonbiblical sources on Judaism and the life and customs in Palestine at the time of Christ are also helpful. Finally, a correct interpretation of a parable will always be consistent with the overall teachings of Jesus.

If the parable has an obvious climax, then its principal message will be closely related to that climax. Usually, an important lesson can be drawn from each of the principal characters or elements of the story, as is clear in the parable of the prodigal son, where each of the three major characters plays a quite different role. Attaching significant spiritual or theological truth to subsidiary details of a story can be misleading and should be avoided. For example, many parables teach about God and his dealings with people through examples of relationships between finite human beings. In such situations, secondary aspects of the comparison will almost always break down, because they will be insufficient and weak representations of an infinite God. In the parable of the wheat and the weeds (Matt. 13:24–30), for instance, the farmer who sowed the seed and later directed the harvest undoubtedly represents God, even though the parable refers to him as being asleep when his enemy sowed weeds in his field. It would be silly to conclude from this that God is unaware of what Satan is doing in the world.

### 4. What Does the Parable Teach about God

Doing the necessary analysis of the parables and digging out their central themes enables us to enjoy the fruits of our studies and to savor the rich truths we discover about God and his relationships with his children. The new insights gained into the character of God from the different pictures of him presented in the parables will amaze us. We will see God as one who opens his door to us to meet our needs and as one who spares nothing to seek the lost and straying and rejoices over their return. We will see him as a God who provides justice to the oppressed who pray to him, as one who justifies those who humbly seek him but rejects the spiritually proud, and as a God who is generous in dispensing gifts and grace to the undeserving.

### 5. What Does the Parable Teach Us about Ourselves

How can Jesus' parables spoken to people in Palestine in the first century A.D. have any meaning or relevance for us today? Can the applications be transferred through time and space to our vastly different situations? Jesus in his divine omniscience understood humanity thoroughly and addressed the essence of the human condition in his teaching—that human standards of righteousness are not God's standards. Our basic problems have not changed with time, only the outward circumstances. We still have neighbors in need, moneylenders and debtors, rich and poor, widows needing justice, religious hypocrites, sons who rebel and leave home, jealous siblings, and irresponsible administrators.

Human nature and tendencies are still very much the same today as they were in Jesus' day. Pride, selfishness, self-indulgence, jealousy, self-righteousness, preoccupation with material concerns rather than the spiritual, unwillingness to forgive, lack of mercy and kindness—these are all character traits identified in Jesus' parables as incompatible with citizenship in the kingdom of heaven. Recognize any of them? We still fight the same battles, don't we? We are challenged as we study Jesus' stories to ask ourselves, "Am I the one?" Yes, the parables remain relevant. They confront us with sobering, unflattering pictures of ourselves in such penetrating realism that we cannot escape their impact. Their message can hit home like a ton of bricks; that is why their study is so exciting and profitable.

# 2

## The Parables of the Patch and the Wineskins

### Primary Scripture Reading

Matthew 9:1–17
Luke 5:36–39

### Supplementary References

Leviticus 4:22–35
Matthew 5:17; 6:1–18;
15:1–20; 23:1–12 and
23–28
Luke 6:1–11
Romans 3:21–24; 13:14
Galatians 3:27; 5:16
Ephesians 6:10–18
Hebrews 10:1–18
Revelation 7:13–14

### Questions for Study and Discussion

1. Read Matthew 9:1–17 and describe each of the Pharisees' objections to Jesus and Jesus' response to them. Explain the additional disputes that Luke records following these parables (Luke 6:1–11).

2. Scan the following passages in which Jesus analyzes the actions of Pharisees: Matthew 6:1–18; 15:1–20; 23:1–12; 23:23–28. Express in your own words what Jesus thought about the Pharisees' motives and actions in their service and worship of God.

3.  Read Leviticus 4:22–35 and explain the symbolism of the sin offerings described in this passage.

    How would performing such a sacrifice make a person feel, do you think?

4.  According to Hebrews 10:1–18, why were animal sacrifices required by God in the Old Testament and on what basis were they acceptable to him?

    What did Jesus mean when he said in Matthew 5:17, "Do not think that I have come to abolish the Law or the Prophets; I have not come to abolish them but to fulfill them"?

5.  Describe the connection you see between verses 10 and 15 of Matthew 9.

    Why didn't Jesus and his disciples fast?

6.  Judging from their context in Matthew 9, what is the main point of the parables of the patch and the wineskins?

    State what you think is symbolized by the old wineskins, the new wine, and the new wineskins.

7.  If our righteous acts are only "filthy rags" (Isa. 64:6), and if we can't patch them up to make them presentable, how can we ever be acceptable to God? (See Rom. 3:21–24; 13:14; Gal. 3:27; Rev. 7:13–14.)

8. From your experience or observations, how can too many "dos and don'ts" hinder true faith?

Give your view of the proper role of good works and exemplary living in the life of a Christian.

How can you make yourself more open to the transforming work of the Word and the Spirit in your life? (See Gal. 5:16–26 and Eph. 6:10–18.)

*I* was raised in a parsonage. Our house was right next door to the church my dad served as pastor. Growing up in such a home is a bit like living in a goldfish bowl. Our home had a constant stream of callers and visitors, so that our family and the way we lived were highly visible both to the congregation and to the small town in which we lived. In that kind of situation it is very easy to fall into the trap of doing the "right" things and "being good" for the wrong reasons, and I was not immune to this tendency. It was easy for me to develop a hypocritical attitude and to make my actions look good from the outside. One particular warning we children often heard as a behavioral reminder was, "What will people think if you do that?"

Fortunately for us, there was a lot of love in our home, expressed especially well by our mother. She made us feel the importance of our father's ministry and made us want to avoid doing things that would hinder it. Her gentle balance between letting us grow up as normal kids while making us aware of our responsibilities as members of the pastor's family had a powerful effect on us. We kids didn't want to hurt or disappoint our parents, for we knew how much they loved us. Their expressions of love and concern for us gave reality and meaning to the daily doses of Bible reading and prayer in our home. Looking back, it's clear to me that feeling our parents' love and seeing their genuine faith lived out in practical ways day after day in our home were important factors in keeping all nine of us from rebelling against our constraints, as preachers' kids sometimes do.

The Pharisees of Jesus' day were very conscious of the question, What will people think? This is evident from such passages as Matthew 6:1–18 and Matthew 23. Their contemporaries no doubt considered them to be as devout and righteous as anyone could be, for they made it a priority to be meticulous in their observance of religious laws. They prayed at certain set times every day, stopping whatever they were doing and wherever they were to stand and pray. They wore prayer shawls with fringes of a certain length, special caps, and phylacteries containing Scripture verses. They fasted twice a week. They avoided eating with "sinners," they prepared their food in strict adherence to "kosher" (proper) practices, and they never ate without a ceremonial washing of their hands. They devoted themselves to the study of both the written Law of the Torah and the oral laws handed down by tradition. In fact, the Pharisees appeared to keep these laws far more diligently than Jesus did and criticized him for what they considered to be his lax observance of religious law.

Jesus' interactions and disputes with the Pharisees over the observance of the laws and traditions of Judaism were frequent and bitter. The parables of the patch and the wineskins, as recorded by Matthew, followed two confrontations, and Luke added two more after the parables. Jesus was accused of blasphemy and of eating with sinners (Matt. 9:1–13), and he was reproached twice for violating the rules for Sabbath observance (Luke 6:1–11). Much of Jesus' teaching and many of his parables are best understood in the light of these disputes.

Because the Pharisees figure so prominently in Jesus' ministry, it is helpful to look into their religious beliefs and practices, as well as their place in Jewish society. In addition, the Pharisees' bent toward self-righteousness, spiritual pride, and a legalistic approach to religion is a very common human tendency, so that even today we have much to learn from Jesus' warnings to them.

### The Pharisees

The Pharisees were the dominant element in Judaism at the time of Jesus. Their members were teachers of law and they ran the schools that taught the Torah to Jewish boys. It is entirely possible that Jesus attended a religious school taught by Pharisees. They were respected by the common people, and their views of God, the Scriptures, and the hereafter were closer to those of Jesus than were those of the Sadducees, the other principal religious sect. The Sadducees were an elite, aristocratic group associated with the high-priesthood and the ruling Sanhedrin. In contrast to them, the Pharisees believed in life after death and accepted the oral traditions handed down from previous generations as inspired by God and morally binding. They spoke for the majority of the Jews, and their religious teachings and customs were widely accepted.

The Pharisees might well be called the Bible-believing fundamentalists of their day. They attempted to apply the God-given Mosiac laws to every aspect of their lives. To do this, they developed the concept of the oral law, which was intended to be a logical extension of the principles of the Mosaic law to any given new situation not covered by the ancient original law. These new applications were supplemented by each generation of scribe-scholars who spent their lives studying and discussing the Torah and the conclusions of prior scribes. The pronouncements of the scribes were memorized and transmitted orally from generation to generation as the tradition of the elders. The blind loyalty of the Pharisees to these oral traditions made them suspicious and resistant to anyone, such as Jesus, who would dare to question these man-made extensions and interpretations of the Mosaic law.

The Pharisees in the main were not hypocrites in the usual sense of that word. Nicodemus was a Pharisee who came seeking Jesus (John 3:1), and the apostle Paul claimed before the Sanhedrin that he was "a Pharisee, the son of a Pharisee" (Acts 23:6). The Pharisees may have been misled by their religious zeal into a false conception of what constituted righteousness, but many were sincere in their error. They were, in fact, so intent on keeping the Mosaic laws that they developed rules and interpretations that would fence them off from even coming close to violating them. These "fence laws" were applied to every conceivable situation and defined what Pharisees could and could not do. For example, the Mosaic law said: "Remember the Sabbath day by keeping it holy. Six days you shall labor and do all your work" (Exod. 20:8). But what constitutes "work"? The fence laws helped out by specifying exactly what could and could not be done on the Sabbath, such as how much weight could be lifted and how far one could walk outside one's house. Even today, orthodox Jews will not carry money on the Sabbath because that is considered work, although there no doubt are ways to circumvent some of these rigid rules. The biblical command "Do not cook a young goat in its mother's milk" (Exod. 23:19) led over time to fence laws that specified kosher cooking procedures requiring completely separate sets of utensils for preparing meat and dairy dishes.

The concept of fence laws may seem strange to us, but don't we Christians sometimes do the same thing when we reduce the very basic commands of God to specific, legalistic sets of "dos and don'ts"? American Protestantism, especially in the past, has been beset by these same tendencies to set up fence laws and with exactly the same dangers. The New Testament warns against drunkenness, so to be safe rather than sorry many Protestants insisted on total abstinence as a tenet of their religion. Movies and dancing of all types were forbidden by some Christian groups because they were "worldly" and might lead to greater sin. Dice and playing cards were not allowed in many homes because they were devices used by gamblers, and it was thought best to banish them entirely to avoid that temptation.

Having such prohibitions may not be all bad, for avoidance of some of these practices may be desirable for a number of very practical reasons. The problem comes when we lose sight of what Jesus taught in Matthew 5 and 6, when he showed by example after example that the essence of sinning lies in one's attitude and not just in the final action. It's always easier to define religion in terms of explicit sets of rules than it is to apply honestly God's standards to our inner attitudes, motives, and purity. We make the same error the Pharisees made when we observe certain practices and prohibitions and then assume that these actions constitute righteousness and godliness, as well as standards to apply both to ourselves and to others against which our faith, orthodoxy, and relationship with God may be judged.

On the other hand, we may do well to examine our weaknesses and temptations and then choose to set up certain prohibitions or positive actions to help us discipline ourselves. For example, we may choose not to watch R- or X-rated movies, we may refrain from certain weekday activities on Sunday to make it a special day, we may set up an early morning hour for our devotions, or we may decide to take part in some social action. However, whatever we do that we find helpful, these things are to be considered our personal expressions of thankfulness to God for his love and grace already received through Christ, rather than demonstrations of our righteousness by which we wish to earn God's favor.

In their zealous determination to keep their oral laws, the Pharisees lost sight of the beautiful intent of the original law of God, which was to show his chosen people his flawless character and to reveal to them their sin, rebellion, and guilt. The ceremonies and sacrifices they were commanded to observe should have reinforced this awareness of sin as well as provided them with an overwhelming sense of God's mercy, forgiveness, and cleansing. Instead, the Pharisees' preoccupation with their myriad religious laws shielded them from seeing the true holiness of God and their own unworthy condition. They equated the keeping of their laws and traditions with righteousness and obedience to God. On this basis, they were righteous and Jesus was not. And this was where most of their conflicts with Jesus arose, for Jesus objected strongly when the Pharisees criticized him or his disciples for infractions of their manmade extensions of God's laws.

Ponder for a moment what Jesus would say to us today if he were warning us against our pharisaical tendencies. He probably would say many of the same things he said to the Pharisees in Matthew 5 and 6. Try to answer these questions paraphrased from those chapters: When you ask forgiveness from God for something you did, are you careful first to make sure you have forgiven those who may have offended you (5:23–24)? Do you avoid actual adultery but indulge in lustful thoughts (5:28)? Do you pray for people you don't like and for those who may have hurt you in some way (5:44)? When you help the needy, do you make sure others know about it (6:2–4)? Do you pray aloud in groups or in church and play the role of a "spiritual leader" while at the same time you neglect your own private prayer time (6:5–6)? The importance of questions such as these is to reveal to us that "nothing good lives in me" (Rom. 7:18), and that only through the sanctifying power of the Spirit

of Christ working in us can our righteousness exceed that
of the Pharisees (Matt. 5:20).

## The Context of the Parables

The short parables of the patch and the wineskins are
surrounded by accounts of Jesus' continuing difficulties
with the Pharisees. Just before he spoke these parables, Jesus
had called Matthew, a tax collector, to follow him and
become his disciple (Luke 5:27–32). Tax collectors were
despised by the Jews because they worked as subcontrac-
tors for the hated Romans. They were considered traitors
to God's chosen people—sinners who were to be excluded
from the synagogue and much of Jewish social life.

Matthew, however, was so overjoyed at being asked to
be a disciple of this great teacher that he couldn't keep his
excitement to himself. He decided to hold a large dinner
party in Jesus' honor and invite all his old friends and
acquaintances so they could meet his wonderful new
friend. When the Pharisees saw that Jesus and his disciples
accepted this invitation and actually sat down and ate with
Matthew and his guests, they were shocked and com-
plained to his disciples, "Why do you eat and drink with
tax collectors and 'sinners'?" This was something no self-
respecting Pharisee would even think of doing.

Jesus was aware that this was not a sincere question, for
he replied with biting sarcasm, "It is not the healthy who
need a doctor, but the sick. But go and learn what this
means: 'I desire mercy, not sacrifice.' For I have not come
to call the righteous, but sinners." What irony! What truth!
How could they fail to catch his meaning? Those who considered themselves righteous did not respond to the call of
the Savior, for they felt no need to be rescued. It was the
outcast sinners and despised tax collectors, those shunned
by the Pharisees, who humbly recognized their need and
sought help. Because Jesus associated with these so-called

sinners and ministered to them, the Pharisees identified him as one of them—a sinner. Guilt by association—how illogical! Jesus was exhibiting the mercy and concern for humankind that is at the heart of true observance of God's law.

Another sharp distinction between Jesus and the Pharisees arose over the question of fasting asked by the disciples of John the Baptist (Matt. 9:14–15), who may have been prompted by the mutterings of the Pharisees to ask it. They asked, "How is it that we and the Pharisees fast, but your disciples do not fast?" Jesus replied with a penetrating question of his own: "How can the guests of the bridegroom mourn while he is with them? The time will come when the bridegroom will be taken from them; then they will fast."

Jesus was telling them that this was not the proper time for his disciples to fast. Fasting should be done for a purpose, not out of formality. In the Pentateuch, the only fast commanded by God was to "deny yourself" on the Day of Atonement (Lev. 23:27). The Jews themselves over the years had added several more fast days to commemorate or mourn special historical events such as the destruction of Jerusalem (Zech. 7:5; 8:19). By the time of Jesus, the more devout Pharisees fasted twice a week—on Mondays and Thursdays. It should be noted that Jesus did not criticize the Pharisees or the disciples of John for fasting, if that was what they wanted to do, but he objected to their attempt to judge him and his disciples on the basis of fasting when fasting served no purpose for them. This was the disciples' time to celebrate Jesus' presence, as Matthew had done. It was a time to feast on the words of life that came from Jesus' lips. This was a time for discovery, learning, and fellowship with their master—an exciting, happy time. A wedding celebration continues for only a little while, then the bridegroom leaves. So with Jesus, for his departure would come soon enough. Jesus was about to complete his mission of bringing into the world a new dispensation of God's love and grace, one which could not be contained within the rigid, legalistic mass of rules into which Judaism had degenerated. The religion of the Pharisees needed a total overhaul, not just a few patches. Jesus then proceeded to illustrate this incompatibility with two short parables.

### The Two Parables

> No one sews a patch of unshrunk cloth on an old garment, for the patch will pull away from the garment, making the tear worse. Neither do men pour new wine into old wineskins. If they do, the skins will burst, the wine will run out and the wineskins will be ruined. No, they pour new wine into new wineskins, and both are preserved (Matt. 9:16–17).

The example of the patch is easily visualized, even though patching is much less common today than it used to be because of our improved fabrics and because our affluent society tends to discard worn clothing rather than repair it. On the other hand, using animal skins in making wine is entirely foreign to our experience, though it was very common in the first century A.D. To make wine, the juice squeezed out of the grapes was poured into a bag made of the skin of an animal, usually a sheep or a goat, which was covered on the outside with pitch or tar to render it less porous to air. The neck of the bag was tied fairly tightly and the juice allowed to ferment. During fermentation grape sugars are converted to alcohol and carbon dioxide gas. The evolved gas created pressure inside the bag which expanded and stretched it. The pressure of the gas also forced it to seep out slowly through the tied neck of the bag and kept air from diffusing back into the bag, which would sour the wine by allowing acids to be formed. The fermentation was essentially complete within three or four days, at which time most of the sugar was used up and the alcohol content increased enough to deactivate the yeast. The new wine could then be poured into jars for use or bottled for aging.

It was important to use new wineskins for making wine because they were pliable and somewhat elastic and could withstand the pressure and the stretching. Used wineskins that had been allowed to dry would have lost their natural oils and elasticity and would likely tear or split if reused and again subjected to the pressure and expansion of the fermentation process.

Do you think the Pharisees recognized themselves in these parables? Don't you imagine they would have caught on pretty quickly that the message Jesus was preaching and demonstrating by his lifestyle was incompatible with their inflexible approach to worshiping God, and that what he proposed was not a patch-up job on Judaism with a few reforms here and there but a whole new and radically different approach to God that did not depend upon careful observance of man-made laws, fasting, and rituals? Did not the old, dried-out wineskins point to their unbending, self-righteous approach to religion that refused to change and would not accommodate the life-changing dynamic of the new message of inner righteousness that Jesus was bringing? And did not the new wineskins symbolize a whole new approach to God that would begin with acknowledgment of sin, humble repentance, and the prayer of the tax collector who cried out: "God, have mercy on me, a sinner"? Because the Pharisees failed to see God's holiness, they failed to perceive their own unworthy condition before his holy law. They were proudly boastful of their efforts to keep the law rather than silenced before it. They did not possess Paul's insight when he wrote:

> Now we know that whatever the law says, it says to those who are under the law, so that every mouth may be silenced and the whole world held accountable to God. Therefore

no one will be declared righteous in his sight by observing the law; rather, through the law we become conscious of sin (Rom. 3:19–20).

The Pharisees couldn't conceive of the possibility that Jesus was the Messiah sent by God to reveal a new phase of his relationship with his people. They refused to believe that Jesus was the fulfillment of their laws and ceremonies, as he himself claimed (Matt. 5:17), or that he was the "Lamb of God who takes away the sins of the world" as testified by John the Baptist (John 1:29). The Pharisees, like all of us, needed to be turned around and reoriented, but they were too set in their ways and too much like used wineskins—dried out and stiff—to do that. Jesus' ironic observation in Luke 5:39, "No one after drinking old wine wants the new, for he says, 'The old is better'," described the Pharisees exactly. They were content with their traditions and refused to consider trying the new wine of the kingdom Jesus was bringing, though the new in this case was better.

Jesus' ultimate mission was to offer to the Pharisees as well as to all mankind a righteousness obtained not by keeping the law but by faith in himself. The apostle Paul stated this clearly:

But now a righteousness from God, apart from the law, has been made known, to which the Law and the Prophets testify. This righteousness from God comes through faith in Jesus Christ to all who believe. . . . God presented him as a sacrifice of atonement, through faith in his blood. . . . Where, then, is boasting? It is excluded. On what principle? On that of observing the law? No, but on that of faith (Rom. 3:21–27).

Are we, like the Pharisees, hanging on to our old, worn-out, patched religious garments—those filthy rags that represent our attempts to appear righteous before God in our own strength and by our own ideas of how to meet his standards? Are we willing to accept the new clothing which Christ offers—his righteousness (Rom. 13:14; Gal. 3:26–27)?

As wine ferments, it stretches its container and tests its flexibility. When we accept Christ, he begins to live within us and to stretch and test us by his purifying work. Are we ready to expand to accommodate new attitudes, goals, and desires, and to do things for him (with his help) that we never thought we could do? Our old rigid ideas and self-made standards will not be able to withstand the dynamic transforming power of the Spirit. What fixed, preconceived ideas, practices, or prejudices are so ingrained in us that we cannot let Christ come into our lives to change and renew us? Do we believe God's Word when it says, "If anyone is in Christ, he is a new creation; the old has gone, the new has come" (2 Cor. 5:17)? Are we holding on to some past stale religious experience and letting that stop any fresh growth and development in our walk with God? Jesus is eager to make us his new creations and to come to live and work within us to help us grow and change. He came to give us an abundant, joyful, exciting new life, but are we willing to be stretched like new wineskins?

# 3

## The Parable of the Sower

### Primary Scripture Reading

Matthew 13:1–23
Mark 4:1–20
Luke 8:4–15

### Supplementary References

Matthew 3:8; 7:15–20
Mark 2, 3
John 15:1–8
Romans 7:4–5
Galatians 5:22–23
Philippians 1:9–11
Colossians 1:6, 9–10

### Questions for Study and Discussion

1.  As background for the parable of the sower, read Mark 2 and 3. What evidences do you see for Jesus' popularity at this time?

    Observe the vastly different responses to his teaching and miracles. How do you explain these differences?

2.  Read the parable of the sower in Matthew 13, Mark 4, and Luke 8. Who met with Jesus after he finished speaking to the large crowd, and what did they ask him?

3. In your own words, explain Jesus' answer to the disciples' question, "Why do you speak to the people in parables?"

   How does this answer relate to people's different responses to him (question 1)?

4. Using Matthew's account of the parable and Jesus' explanation, prepare and fill in the following chart (on a separate sheet of paper):

| Type of soil | What happened to seed? | Jesus' interpretation | How did it apply to crowd at seashore? | Possible application to me today |
|---|---|---|---|---|
| Hard (Path) | | | | |
| Rocky (Shallow) | | | | |
| Thorny (Weedy) | | | | |
| Good | | | | |

5. List the different meanings of *thorns* from all three accounts of the parable.

   What are your most troublesome thorns?

6. In your opinion, what is the meaning of *fruit* in the parable? (For other references to fruit, see Matthew 3:8; 7:15–20; John 15:1–8; Romans 7:4–5; Galatians 5:22–23; Philippians 1:9–11; Colossians 1:6, 9–10.)

7. Give a one-sentence description of how, you think, each manifestation of the fruit of the Spirit given in Galatians 5:22 should be expressed in the life of a Christian.

   What can you do to make the soil of your heart more fruitful?

*G*arage sales fascinate me. There's no telling what interesting things I might find. Several years ago I bought an iron wedge perfect for splitting logs. At another sale I picked up an old-fashioned, hand-cranked coffee grinder that could also be used to grind cornmeal. I also found a large pick axe at a bargain price because the handle was split. But the find that excited me most was a hand-held grass seeder, which I felt I really needed. My wife complains that I've never used most of these items, which I confess is true, but I maintain one never knows when they will come in handy. I rest my case on the seeder, which I used several times before it fell apart.

My seeder consisted of a canvas bag which hung from my neck. The seed flowed from this bag into an attached box onto which a crank was mounted. The crank turned a fan-like blade inside the box which scattered the seed in a wide arc in front of me as I walked along. Perhaps it was too windy the first time I used the seeder, for seed flew everywhere. A lot went on the lawn, where I wanted it to go, but some landed on the sidewalk and driveway. Other seed blew into my wife's flower bed (I heard about that for a long time), and some wound up in the ivy vines growing alongside the house. But the seeder did serve a purpose: I gained a lot of sympathy for the farmer in the parable of the sower whose seed did not all fall on good soil.

### The Context of the Parable

It was about the middle of his three years of public ministry when Jesus told this parable. Jesus' popularity was near its peak, for he was attracting large crowds every day. But opposition to him from the religious leaders was also increasing. In fact, Mark lists five confrontations in the two chapters immediately preceding the parable. These were serious clashes, not just disagreements on minor doctrinal points, for Mark writes: "The Pharisees went out and began to plot with the Herodians how they might kill Jesus" (3:6). The persistent unbelief of these religious leaders is a very fitting backdrop to the message of the parable of the sower and to Jesus' answer to the disciples' question about why he was speaking in parables.

### The Setting of the Parable

That same day Jesus went out of the house and sat by the lake. Such large crowds gathered around him that he got into a boat and sat in it, while all the people stood on the shore. Then he told them many things in parables, saying: "A farmer went out to sow his seed" (Matt. 13:1–3).

It's hard for us to grasp the pressure on Jesus at this point in his ministry. He seems to have had little respite from the crowds that surged around him day after day. Even when he left the house where he had been teaching to go to the lake, the people followed him, eager to hear more. At the lake Jesus got into a boat and the crowd gathered expectantly along the shore. I wonder what Jesus was thinking as he saw all those people and prepared to speak to them. He knew, of course, that people had come there for a variety of reasons. Many were truly interested in what he had to say—genuine seekers after truth who wanted to find out if he was really the promised Messiah. Others were merely curious, following the latest fad, not wanting to miss out on the current hot topic of conversation. Still others, he knew, came with their minds already made up. They were there with critical ears and were listening for something with which to accuse him and support the charges they planned to bring against him.

I enjoy speculating that, at the moment Jesus was thinking about the attitudes of the people seated before him, his eye caught sight of a farmer in the distance scattering seed as he walked along in his field. The aptness of that scene to his listeners provided the perfect example with which to teach and to challenge them to examine their response to his words.

## The Parable

A farmer went out to sow his seed. As he was scattering the seed, some fell along the path, and the birds came and ate it up. Some fell on rocky places, where it did not have much soil. It sprang up quickly, because the soil was shallow. But when the sun came up, the plants were scorched, and they withered because they had no root. Other seed fell among thorns, which grew up and choked the plants. Still other seed fell on good soil, where it produced a crop—a hundred, sixty or thirty times what was sown. He who has ears, let him hear (Matt. 13:3–9).

The picture presented in this parable was very easy for Jesus' listeners to understand. They probably had either sown seed themselves or had watched it being sown. At that time it was customary for the sower to carry a sack of seed at his waist and walk back and forth through his field scattering handfuls of seed in an arc ahead of him by sweeping his hand from side to side. With practice, the seeding could be done fairly evenly. Historians tell us that the farmer of that day would sow first and then plow. He would not plow nearly as deeply as do our mechanized present-day farmers, but just deeply enough to imbed the seed in the soil. Because the farmer might not remember exactly where the rocky substrate was too close to the surface to allow the seed to take root and find water, some seed would fall inadvertently on these areas. Furthermore, since Palestine is quite hilly, the fields were usually narrow and irregular in shape. They were often bordered on one side by paths for pedestrians and for shepherds and their flocks. Frequently, the other side of the field would border a steep hillside which would be left untilled and used for grazing. Jesus' parable fits this situation exactly. In spite of the sower's efforts to sow only the areas of good soil that would be plowed, some of his seed fell on the hard packed path. Other seed ended up where the ground was thin because of the underlying rock, and some fell near the hillside where competing grass and weeds had already taken root.

Jesus ended his parable with the words, "He that has ears to hear, let him hear" (v. 9), challenging his listeners to go home and ponder the meaning of the "many things" he had taught them. But some lingered to ask questions.

## The Disciples' Questions

The disciples were apparently bothered by Jesus' increased use of parables at this time and, besides that, they were not sure what this parable meant. After most of the crowd had gone, they came to Jesus and asked, "Why do you speak to the people in parables?" (v. 10). Jesus replied:

> The knowledge of the secrets of the Kingdom of heaven has been given to you, but not to them. Whoever has will be given more, and he will have an abundance. Whoever does not have, even what he has will be taken from him. This is why I speak to them in parables: "Though seeing, they do not see; though hearing, they do not hear or understand" (Matt. 13:11–13).

What a strange answer! Wasn't Jesus trying to reach and convert everyone in his audience? Didn't Jesus say clearly to Zaccheaus that "the Son of Man came to seek and to save what was lost" (Luke 19:10)? Surely that applied to all who sincerely sought him. But Jesus was also realistic; he knew the condition of the hearts of his audience. His situation was like that of Isaiah, who was charged by God to deliver his message to the people but at the same time warned by God that they would not listen because their hearts were calloused, their ears dulled, and their eyes blinded due to their unbelief (Isa. 6:8–13).

Jesus' answer to the disciples' question encompassed both God's sovereignty and man's responsibility. He knew that in God's eternal plan of redemption his own people, as a nation, would reject him and his message, as foretold in the Old Testament. This he accepted. Yet he continued to preach to them, even that very day urging them to open their ears to his message. Later, he showed his great concern and sorrow for his people by weeping over Jerusalem (Luke 13:34 and 19:41–43). He grieved for them because the glorious message of the kingdom that would have brought them real peace was now hidden from their eyes because of their persistent rejection. At the same time, for those with open minds and hearts, Jesus' teachings and parables took on new meaning as they listened and understood more and more the "secrets of the kingdom" (Matt. 13:11). (See also chapter 1, p. 25, of this study.)

Jesus then answered the disciples' other question about the meaning of the parable in such a brief, straightforward way that they probably wondered why they hadn't figured it out for themselves.

> Listen then to what the parable of the sower means: When anyone hears the message about the kingdom and does not understand it, the evil one comes and snatches away what was sown in his heart. This is the seed sown along the path. The one who received the seed that fell on rocky places is the man who hears the word and at once receives it with joy. But since he has no root, he lasts only a short time. When trouble or persecution comes because of the word, he quickly falls away. The one who received the seed that fell among thorns is the man who hears the word, but the worries of this life and the deceitfulness of wealth choke it, making it unfruitful. But the one who received the seed that fell on good soil is the man who hears the word and understands it. He produces a crop, yielding a hundred, sixty or thirty times what was sown (Matt. 13:18–23).

How brilliantly the parable describes the varying responses to Jesus' words! The explanation is not forced or far-fetched; it is simple, natural, and entirely fitting to the narrative. It is not complex or overly allegorical. Jesus said almost nothing about the sower and the seed, and very little about the fruit. He concentrated on only one aspect of the story—the condition of the soils and the discriminating effect this has on the seed falling on it. Jesus identified the seed as the message of the kingdom that he was bringing (v. 19) and the soils as people who hear the message and respond to it in different ways. Jesus' clear explanation was one that would stick in their minds for a long time.

## The Sower

Who is the sower? Though the sower is not emphasized in Jesus' interpretation of the parable, he apparently identifies himself as the sower (vv. 16–17) who is bringing the long-awaited message from God to his people. Thus, the parable is an autobiographical story depicting Jesus' own experience as he presented his message to his countrymen and observed their responses. Recalling this parable would have been a great comfort to the disciples as Jesus' ministry progressed and antagonism to him increased. Many would not listen to Jesus' message; many would seem to be interested, only to fall away later. But the promise of the parable was that when the word was sown it would bring forth a fruitful harvest. Don't we observe exactly the same responses to the gospel today that Jesus described in his parable?

The Scriptures are clear that we as Christians are to be busily engaged in planting seed. The Great Commission (Matt. 28:18–20), for example, states this plainly. Our responsibility is to make sure that the seed we sow is good, which means that our message is clear, compelling, and consistent with God's Word. How can we do this? Only through prayer that God will first give us understanding of his Word as we study it and then prepare the heartsoil onto which our seed will fall. It is the work of the Holy Spirit to prepare the soil and to generate life from the seed. The parable teaches that we should not be discouraged if we fail to see immediate results. The church's role is to be ready to nurture and care for any young, sprouting plants so that their initial response can grow to maturity and fruitfulness (Eph. 4:12–13).

## The Soils

The soils in the parable are the hearers of the message of the kingdom. That's all of us! God has spoken and through his Word is now speaking to us. How do we respond? Which of the soils describes us?

### The Hard Soil (the path)

In Jesus' interpretation, the hard-beaten pathway illustrates those who hear the word but will not let its truth penetrate their minds. The word is heard superficially and is then easily displaced by other thoughts, impulses, or desires. The Pharisees and scribes were the most glaring example of this type of hearer. These religious leaders had closed their minds to Jesus and refused even to consider the possibility that he was a prophet sent from God, let alone the Messiah. Even though they witnessed his miracles, his message could not penetrate the thick layer of spiritual pride that surrounded their minds and consciences and made them unable to see that their all-consuming approach to worshiping and serving God, centered on externalities, often caused them to miss the point of the commandments.

But were the Pharisees so different from many of us today? Don't we Christians have the same tendencies? It's easy to point fingers at them, but have we considered our own responses to God's Word? Don't we often close our minds to what God reveals from his Word to us? Have you, like me, read or heard Jesus' command to "love one another, even as I have loved you" so many times that its real meaning fails to sink in and condemn us when we continue to dislike and avoid some of our fellow believers? How can we recite "Blessed are the peacemakers" and then through unkind criticism and gossip sow dissention in our own church?

We know by rote the commandment "Thou shalt not steal," and yet we find ways to excuse ourselves for cheating on our income tax or for taking home for our personal use little items that belong to our employer. If we continue to hear the Word over and over and do not let its message sink in, convict us, and change us, then we, too, have become like the hard soil—impenetrable and closed to the truth.

## The Rocky Soil

Jesus likened the rocky soil to the person who hears the word and responds to it immediately and joyfully, perhaps caught up with others in the emotion of the moment. But the response is superficial and shallow, so when "trouble or persecution comes because of the word, he quickly falls away" (Matt. 13:21). Changes in lifestyle and interests brought about by new convictions based on God's Word can evoke snide comments and criticism from family, friends, or coworkers. Like plants in shallow soil, those whose convictions are not deeply rooted will not be able to stand the heat, and their interest will wither. Many in Jesus' day who were initially interested in his message and "heard him gladly" (Mark 12:37 KJV) later turned away. They were excited about Jesus' signs and miracles and even wanted to make him king after he fed a crowd of five thousand from five loaves and two fish (John 6:14–15), but gradually these same people came to realize that the kingdom Jesus kept talking about was not what they had been looking for. It was hard for them to accept Jesus' metaphor that he was the Bread of Life (John 6:32–59). That was not the kind of bread they wanted, so "from this time many . . . turned back and no longer followed him" (John 6:66).

The picture John painted of the many who forsook Jesus and the few who remained true to him stirs our hearts. We feel sure we would have been among those who remained true. Or would we? How many times have we been stirred and convicted by a compelling sermon or Bible lesson and resolved to do something about some failure or weakness in our lives, only to have our resolve quickly fizzle out like a damp firecracker when we returned to our daily routines? This has happened to me more times than I care to admit. We need these emotional responses to God's truth; they are the work of the Spirit. But they are meant to take root in actions and changes in conduct that continue. This is the lasting response that Jesus desires for us and creates in us as we pray.

### The Weedy Soil

Jesus identified the weedy, thorny soil with the one who hears the word but is so bound up with the affairs and concerns of this life that any growth from the word gets choked off and never develops to the point of bearing fruit. Taken together, the three Gospels list "the worries of this life," "the deceitfulness of wealth," "the desires for other things," and "pleasures" as the main competitors to the growth of the word in us.

In Jesus' audience, the weedy soil represented those who were intrigued by his teaching but were just too busy and too interested in other things to make a real commitment to him. Even as he spoke, their thoughts may have strayed to family problems, their next vacation, unfinished work at home, something they wanted to buy, or an upcoming business deal. Doesn't Jesus' expression "the deceitfulness of wealth" (Matt. 13:22) hit home to us today? The pull of material things is very subtle. It's enlightening to tabulate how much of our time and energy in any given week is devoted to the affairs of life, material things, and pleasures and to compare that to the time spent meditating on God and his Word. These distracting weeds consume our thoughts, weaken and crowd out spiritual growth, and prevent new growth in our lives.

Jesus also warned that "the worries of this life" (v. 22) can weaken and defeat the effect of his message. Worry can become our prevailing attitude, regardless of age or situation. Problems, troubles, and even disasters are a real possibility for all of us, and they can defeat us if we let them concern or consume us so much that they crowd out our view of the Son who can bring light, hope, peace, and joy in the midst of trials. Remember, you are invited to "cast all your anxiety on him because he cares for you"

(1 Peter 5:7). It is not a sin to worry, but it is a sin not to take our worries to the Lord.

Some years ago when I was a young university professor worried about gaining tenure and earning promotions through the faculty ranks, I felt a real tension between the demands of my career to teach and produce significant research and publications and my commitments to my family and to the Lord. I was well aware that some of my colleagues worked in their offices or laboratories most weekends, and I didn't see how I could compete if I took off time to be a husband and father in addition to being active in our church. This tension drove me to pray daily for wisdom in setting priorities for that day and for efficiency in the use of my time. As I shared my worries and concerns with the Lord, they seemed to lessen, and I was able to function better and with real peace and joy in all three areas.

God doesn't ask us to choose between doing a good job at work, at home, or in our church. What he does ask is that we involve him in all the affairs of our lives, so that whatever we do and in whatever endeavor we are engaged, he leads and guides our decisions and actions. We can then rejoice with him over any successes that come our way and talk to him about our problems and worries. I have found that being conscious of the presence and nearness of God in whatever I am doing—working, relaxing, playing tennis, or visiting with friends—keeps me from going overboard in any one area so that I lose my perspective, get too involved, and crowd out my spiritual growth.

### The Good Soil

Jesus described the good soil simply as one who hears the word, understands it, and then produces a crop many times larger than what was sown. This type of listener avoids the problems of the others. His or her mind is open and receptive, the word penetrates, takes root, and develops without distractions to maturity and fruitfulness. Jesus is emphatic; the real test of good hearing is the fruit which is produced.

The classic passage on fruit bearing is John 15. There Jesus said:

> I am the vine and my Father is the gardener. He cuts off every branch in me that bears no fruit, while every branch that does bear fruit he prunes so that it will be even more fruitful. You are already clean because of the word I have spoken to you. Remain in me, and I will remain in you. No branch can bear fruit by itself; it must remain in the vine. Neither can you bear fruit unless you remain in me.

Jesus' message is that the secret of fruitfulness is to draw strength and nourishment from himself, the living Word, just as branches draw their sustenance from the vine. We do this through fellowship with him through prayer and the study of the Word. By these means and with the help of the Spirit we can be pruned to conform to his standards. Paul describes the fruit which results from abiding in Christ as the "fruit of the Spirit" and lists the characteristics developed in us as follows:

> But the fruit of the Spirit is love, joy, peace, patience, kindness, goodness, faithfulness, gentleness and self-control. Against such things there is no law. Those who belong to Christ Jesus have crucified the sinful nature with its passions and desires (Gal. 5:22–24).

We tend to think of spiritual fruit as reproducing our faith in others by sharing our faith with them and by discipling. But as important as this is, it is not the primary meaning of the term as it is used in the New Testament. The word *fruit* as used in the Gospels and elsewhere in the New Testament almost always refers to a transformation of attitude and character that results from abiding in Christ. The reason for this may be that the New Testament type of fruit exhibited by traits of character is an absolutely necessary prerequisite to effective witnessing. If the fruits of the Spirit are clearly seen in us, e.g., love, joy, kindness, goodness, and gentleness, this will be noticed by others and earn natural opportunities to witness effectively to our faith.

As Christians, our first obligation is to take in the Word, either by hearing or reading, and then to meditate on it so that it can take root, grow, and produce fruitful changes in our lives. God's Word is powerful, but our soil may be deficient—hard, shallow, or weedy. God can change the soil of our hearts to be receptive to the truth of his Word, if we ask him. He can help us root out the weeds and thorns that so easily distract us and prevent us from being fruitful.

Jesus ended his parable by saying, "He who has ears, let him hear" (Matt. 13:9). Do we have ears that hear? Are we listening to Jesus' message? What are we doing about it? The apostle James put the challenge this way:

> Do not merely listen to the word, and so deceive yourselves. Do what it says. Anyone who listens to the word but does not do what it says is like a man who looks at his face in a mirror and, after looking at himself, goes away and immediately forgets what he looks like. But the man who looks intently into the perfect law that gives freedom, and continues to do this, not forgetting what he has heard, but doing it—he will be blessed in what he does (James 1:22–25).

# 4

## Six Parables of the Kingdom

**Primary Scripture Reading**

Matthew 13:24–51

**Supplementary References**

Matthew 4:17; 7:21–23;
18:15–17; 25:31–34
Mark 1:15; 9:1
Luke 17:20–21
John 18:36
1 Cor. 5:1–5
Titus 3:10–11

### Questions for Study and Discussion

1. Group the six parables found in Matthew 13:24–51 into three pairs, each pair having a common theme.

   What theme would you assign to each pair?

2. Why did Jesus tell the disciples the parables of the weeds and the wheat and the dragnet, do you think?

   Based on these two parables, do you think churches today should attempt to weed out those persons who do not give evidence of being true believers? Why or why not? (See also Matt. 18:15–17; 1 Cor. 5:1–5; Titus 3:10–11.)

3. How would the parable of the mustard seed have been an encouragement to the disciples?

   Give some examples of growth of which you are aware that correspond to the lesson of this parable.

4. What, in your opinion, are the parallels between the way yeast works in dough and the way the kingdom of heaven works (a) in individuals and (b) throughout the world?

5. In what ways are the parables of the treasure in the field and the pearl of great value alike, and in what ways do they differ?

   What message do you get from them?

6. Considering all seven kingdom parables in Matthew 13, including that of the sower, what perspective and encouragement would they have given the disciples to help them after Jesus was gone?

7. Read the following references on the kingdom: Matthew 4:17; Mark 1:15; 9:1; Luke 17:20–21; John 18:36. From these passages, what did Jesus imply about when the kingdom would appear and what its nature would be?

   In your own words, try to reconcile these verses with what Jesus taught about the kingdom in Matthew 7:21–23; 25:31–34.

8. From your study of this lesson, what does the term *kingdom of heaven* mean to you?

*T*he kingdom of heaven or its equivalent, the kingdom of God, was a subject Jesus loved to talk about. It was a principal theme of his ministry. He came into the world to inaugurate a new relationship between God and man. Jesus saw the world as belonging to the Father by right of creation, but he also recognized that much of the world had fallen under the influence of Satan, and that, whether people were aware of it or not, many of them were following Satan's leadership rather then God's. The apostle John reflected this view when he wrote, "The whole world is under the control of the evil one" (1 John 5:19).

Even the Jewish religious leaders were accused by Jesus of belonging to their father, the devil (John 8:44). This statement may have shocked his listeners, but it was not a new development. From earliest times those who followed God in faith were a small minority. Out of the fallen world, God called individuals and families, such as Abraham, Isaac, and Jacob, to follow him. God called Jacob's descendants— a weak, insignificant tribe of slaves—to be his chosen people (Deut. 7:6–9) and led them out of Egypt into their promised land. But even these chosen people, whom God led and fed in miraculous ways, rebelled and strayed, preferring the idolatry of their heathen neighbors to the worship of Jehovah God. Again and again God in his mercy called them back to himself and forgave them, but their times of repentance were short-lived (Neh. 9; Acts 7).

It was God's plan that, when the time was right, he would intervene in this situation by sending his Son into the world on a mission of redemption. Jesus would empower a movement that would begin small but would ultimately become a worldwide body of believers rescued from Satan's clutch. Jesus called this revolutionary new movement the kingdom of heaven. It would be empowered not by political or military might but by the death and resurrection of its founder; and its message would be propagated and proclaimed by the least likely of humans—individuals who would be forced to rely on the power of God rather than their own abilities.

Much of what Jesus taught about this kingdom was in the form of parables. Seven of these are assembled in Matthew 13, the first of which we have already studied. The six that are the subject of this chapter appear to fall into three pairs, each pair bringing out a particular aspect of kingdom characteristics.

### The Wheat and the Weeds

I'm not much of a gardener. My wife, on the other hand, loves flowers and has several large flower beds which I help care for. On my own I maintain only one small plot just large enough to grow six or seven tomato plants. Even in our modest beds, we find that weeds are a constant problem and require constant (and discriminating) vigilance to keep them under control. More than once my wife has cried out, "That wasn't a weed you just pulled up. That was a flower!"

In Jesus' day, fields were sown by scattering seeds by hand. The plants would then come up randomly, not in rows and not evenly spaced. Think of how difficult it would be to hoe such a field. No wonder the servants in Jesus' parable were upset when they saw all those weeds in their master's wheat field. What would he do about the weeds? Jesus' audience listened intently as the story unfolded.

Jesus told them another parable: "The kingdom of heaven is like a man who sowed good seed in his field. But while everyone was sleeping, his enemy came and sowed weeds among the wheat, and went away. When the wheat sprouted and formed heads, then the weeds also appeared. The owner's servants came to him and said, 'Sir, didn't you sow good seed in your field? Where then did the weeds come from?' 'An enemy did this,' he replied. The servants asked him, 'Do you want us to go and pull them up?' 'No,' he answered, 'because while you are pulling the weeds, you may root up the wheat with them. Let both grow together until the harvest. At that time I will tell the harvesters: First collect the weeds and tie them in bundles to be burned, then gather the wheat and bring it into my barn'" (Matt. 13:24–30).

Then he left the crowd and went into the house. His disciples came to him and said, "Explain to us the parable of the weeds in the field." He answered, "The one who sowed the good seed is the Son of Man. The field is the world, and the good seed stands for the sons of the kingdom. The weeds are the sons of the evil one, and the enemy who sows them is the devil. The harvest is the end of the age, and the harvesters are angels. As the weeds are pulled up and burned in the fire, so it will be at the end of the age. The Son of Man will send out his angels, and they will weed out of his kingdom everything that causes sin and all who do evil. They will throw them into the fiery furnace, where there will be weeping and gnashing of teeth. Then the righteous will shine like the sun in the kingdom of their Father. He who has ears, let him hear" (Matt. 13:36–43).

The weed in Jesus' parable may have been darnel, a plant that looks a lot like wheat when it is young and growing but whose mature kernels are grayish in color, have a bitter, unpleasant taste, and are slightly poisonous. The presence of darnel in a wheat field would be a serious problem and could result in significant financial loss. Workers would have to be hired to pull up the darnel plants either early or late in the growing season, always with the danger of uprooting the wheat along with it, or else to separate the good from the bad kernels of grain by hand after harvesting them together. Undoubtedly the best and most efficient way to remove the weeds was the one suggested by the owner, for at harvest time any mature wheat plants inadvertently uprooted with the weeds could still be separated and added to the yield.

Jesus explained only two of the six parables—this one and the parable of the dragnet. He explained that he, the Son of Man, is the one who sowed good seed when he came into the world with his kingdom message. The good seed and the wheat growing from it are those who believed in him and accepted his message. The enemy who planted the weeds is the devil, and the weeds are those who bought Satan's line and were committed to him. The harvest is the end of the age when God's angels will gather all people for the final judgment, at which time the wheat will be separated from the weeds and each given their just reward— the evil to everlasting punishment and the righteous to reign with Christ in glory. (See Matt. 25:31–46.)

What would this parable mean to the disciples as they recalled it later? Don't you think it gave them encouragement, perspective, and patience to know that the good seed entrusted to them by Jesus would bring forth a fruitful harvest, even though there was much opposition and many who would not accept their message? And what about us? Aren't we often confused by the profusion and apparent triumph of evil all around us? Don't we long for justice to be done and wonder when God is going to do something about it? The parable teaches that God is in control. He allows good and evil to coexist for a time, but he will ultimately intervene and mete out justice.

Does the parable have anything to say about the church? It baffles many people that there is so much jealousy, selfishness, pride, and even immorality evident in churches today. Is this to be expected and tolerated? Sorry to say, there are hypocrites in the church. Often believers and unbelievers look and act alike, go through the same motions, and are difficult to distinguish because of the presence of sin in both. Does the parable imply that more harm than good may come from attempts to root out those judged to be unbelievers because some young wheat plants may also be uprooted? Can church members or elders be trusted to make such judgments, or should all judgment be left to God?

And what about church discipline? Is not the church instructed elsewhere in the New Testament (Matt. 18:15–17; 1 Cor. 5:1–5; Titus 3:10–11) to protect itself from those who would damage its reputation in the world by gross, immoral acts? Yes, but the Bible also teaches that the purpose of any such confrontation is to win back the wayward one (1 Cor. 5:5; 2 Cor. 2:5–8; Gal. 6:1–2). I have participated in these types of situations as a church officer and found them to be experiences that demanded much prayer, patience, and love. They forced me to examine my own actions, attitudes, and life in order to avoid the sin of spiritual pride warned against in Galatians 6:1–5. The church's message is for sinners, believing or unbelieving, yet its membership is for those who truly commit themselves to Christ in repentance and faith and desire to live as true members of his body.

## The Dragnet

One summer during a family vacation on the Georgia coast, I watched a man and his wife catching fish with a dragnet. Their net, about seventy-five feet long and six feet high, was tied between two poles and had floats along the top and weights on the bottom. One of them would pull one end of the net out into the ocean, walk against the current for ten to twenty yards, and then swing toward shore. Each time they dragged the net onto the beach, it brought up an assortment of sea life, including several good-sized ocean trout. My family noticed how fascinated I was and got together to give me such a net for my next birthday.

What fun we've had with our net! Pulling it up on shore and seeing all the flapping, wriggling creatures is always exciting. We haven't caught any trout so far, but there are always shiny minnows splashing around, a few blue crabs, and occasionally some shrimp. We've also caught several sting rays and once a two-foot sand shark. We usually keep the edible blue crabs and shrimp, but toss back all the rest, in a sense separating the good from the bad, just as in Jesus' parable.

> Once again, the kingdom of heaven is like a net that was let down into the lake and caught all kinds of fish. When it was full, the fishermen pulled it up on shore. Then they sat down and collected the good fish in baskets, but threw the bad away. This is how it will be at the end of the age. The angels will come and separate the wicked from the righteous and throw them into the fiery furnace, where there will be weeping and gnashing of teeth (Matt. 13:47–50).

Good teacher that he was, Jesus again drew his story from everyday life. The dragnet used by commercial fishermen in those days was a large, rectangular net with ropes tied to each corner. With floats attached to the top and heavy weights to the bottom, the net would be attached to poles and dragged behind a boat. As the boat moved forward by being rowed or sailed, the net would trap any sea life swimming in its path. The net was nondiscriminating, so after it was pulled up, the catch would be sorted and separated. Jews were commanded not to eat certain fish (Lev. 10:9–12), so the forbidden fish were removed from the good varieties before the men took the catch to market.

As with its twin parable about the wheat and the tares, Jesus explained that this parable illustrates the judgment and separation that will happen at the end of the age. Apparently, the main point of this short parable is that the message of the kingdom, which Jesus' followers should take to the whole world (Matt. 28:19), would inevitably contact, touch, and attract all kinds of people, both good and bad, sincere and hypocritical. This should not surprise or discourage his followers, for God is sovereign and righteous and will judge everyone fairly in his good time. The certainty of a final judgment is the climax of each of these parables. Paul echoed this certainty when he wrote:

> For we will all stand before God's judgment seat. It is written: "'As surely as I live,' says the Lord, 'every knee will bow before me; every tongue will confess to God.'" So then, each of us will give an account of himself to God (Rom. 14:10–11).

## The Mustard Seed

I'm sure the more Jesus talked about his kingdom, the more the disciples tried to imagine what it would be like. Jesus knew they were confused and that the kingdom he was establishing at this time was altogether different from what they had expected. How could they have imagined that it would start so small, and that it would be brought into being in a very unusual way—by the suffering, death, and apparent defeat of its founder? How could they have anticipated that its first leaders would be eleven very ordinary men whose principal religious training was picked up piecemeal as they walked beside Jesus, talked to him, and listened to him teach in the towns and villages?

If you were part of that group of twelve (counting Judas), and looked around you to appraise honestly and realistically the status of your movement, would you have been encouraged and hopeful? By any human standard their movement looked doomed. Jesus knew they needed encouragement and perspective so they would not despair after he left them, so he told them a simple story that would stick in their minds to describe the present and future status of his kingdom. He wanted them to know they were part of God's plan for the world, and God would work through them to accomplish his will, as unlikely as that appeared at that time.

> He told them another parable: "The kingdom of heaven is like a mustard seed, which a man took and planted in his field. Though it is the smallest of all your seeds, yet when it grows, it is the largest of garden plants and becomes a tree, so that the birds of the air come and perch in its branches" (Matt. 13:31–32).

The mustard seed is the proverbial tiny object—just a speck—and Jesus himself used it that way to describe the power of only a little true faith (Matt. 17:20). Yet, when planted, it grows into a bush as high as ten to twelve feet, with branches big and strong enough for birds to roost and find shelter. The picture of birds finding refuge in a tree would have been familiar to Jesus' Jewish listeners, for the prophet Ezekiel described the glories of Israel as a large cedar tree: "All the birds of the air nested in its boughs . . . all the great nations lived in its shade" (Ezek. 31:6).

Jesus did not interpret this parable, but if we follow the pattern of his interpretation of the wheat and the tares, we can conclude that the man who planted the mustard seed is, again, the Son of Man, the field is the world, the tiny seed is the good news of the coming of the kingdom, and the resulting tree is the eventual visible result of the growth and spread of the kingdom message: a worldwide body of believers who provide a place where people of all nations can find hope and peace. Wouldn't this be an encouraging message for the disciples?

Jesus' choice of the mustard plant for his illustration is interesting. The tiny size of this seed is obviously an important aspect of the story. Yet, if Jesus had wanted to emphasize the eventual large size of the mature plant, why didn't he choose the mighty oak or cedar for his example as Ezekiel did? Perhaps Jesus' choice was deliberate at both ends, and he was saying that the kingdom movement would never be dominant and powerful by earthly standards. That does not seem to be the way God works in the world. Christians have had a tremendous effect on the world, but never because of their dominance, size, or power. In fact, the witness of Christians has always been most effective when they were a weak and sometimes persecuted minority, forced to rely on God for help and strength. Charles Colson is a modern example of this. As a disbarred lawyer and ex-convict, he has had a much greater and more lasting impact on the lives of men and women than when he occupied a position of power close to the presidency.

When I think of the way God works from small beginnings, I think of the influence of a man like Martin Luther and the changes that resulted from his convictions both within and without the organized church of his day. I think also of William Tyndale's translation of the Bible into the language of the people, and the lasting effects of men like John and Charles Wesley in both England and America. In my own experience, both my wife and I have participated in and benefited from Bible Study Fellowship, which was started by Miss A. W. Johnson during the 1950s, some years after she was forced to leave her mission work in China. She began by teaching a class of five women meeting in a living room, not dreaming that God would bless and expand her efforts into a worldwide ministry of nearly one thousand classes meeting on at least six continents, with hundreds of thousands of men and women growing in Christ through its six-year course of Bible study.

How does God accomplish his work from such humble beginnings? The apostle Paul expressed it best: "Therefore, since through God's mercy we have this ministry, we do not lose heart . . . but we have this treasure in jars of clay to show that this all-surpassing power is from God and not from us" (2 Cor. 4:7). It is only as we acknowledge our weakness and dependence on him that God can work through us to accomplish his will. He wants each of us to allow the seed of the gospel of Christ to grow and develop within us, so that we become mustard trees in our own spheres, sharing our faith with those about us. A lot of birds are out there that need to be fed and sheltered spiritually, and God wants each of us to see to their needs.

## The Leaven

While living for a year in the San Francisco area, our family got hooked on sourdough bread. We dreaded the thought of not being able to enjoy this treat after we returned home to the Midwest. Fortunately, a kind neighbor gave us a "starter," a small portion of dough containing the active yeast culture responsible for the distinctive taste, which we could take back with us. It amazed us how little of this special leaven was needed to transform ordinary dough into something special, and we continued to enjoy sourdough bread after we were back home in Indiana.

Jesus' companion parable to that of the mustard seed used leaven, or yeast, to illustrate the way the kingdom grows and spreads.

> He told them still another parable: "The kingdom of heaven is like yeast that a woman took and mixed into a large amount of flour until it worked all through the dough" (Matt. 13:33).

A little leaven goes a long way, we say, referring to the way it permeates and profoundly affects bread dough. Many a cook has been horrified to see the results of for-getting to add yeast or baking powder to the dough mix. Without yeast baked bread is flat, hard, and unappetizing. With yeast it is light, soft, and delicious.

What is Jesus' point here? We know that leaven was something the Jews were told to avoid during the feast of the passover (Exod. 12:17–20), and that the word was used by Jesus (Matt. 16:6) and elsewhere in the New Testament (1 Cor. 5:6–8) to describe the insidious way evil works and spreads. In the present context, however, Jesus seems to use it in a positive way to illustrate the growing and per-meating effects of the kingdom and its message. Whereas the mustard seed points to external, visible growth, the effect of leaven is from within, raising and transforming the raw dough in which it works.

The purpose of the gospel message is to change and transform the world, but first it must change the hearts of individuals. Isn't that God's pattern? Think of how yeast works. The live organisms are added to the dough from the outside; they are not spontaneously generated. If yeast is not added, the dough remains flat and unraised—dead. Perhaps Paul was thinking of this metaphor when he wrote:

> But because of his great love for us, God, who is rich in mercy, made us alive with Christ even when we were dead in transgressions—it is by grace you have been saved. And God raised us up with Christ and seated us with him in the heavenly realms in Christ Jesus, in order that in the com-ing ages he might show the incomparable riches of his grace (Eph. 2:4–7).

When Christ makes us alive spiritually, a transformation takes place within us. Our thought patterns and attitudes are enlivened and changed so that we become sensitive to what God's will is for us and are helped by his Spirit to be willing and able to do it. Paul wrote:

> Don't let the world around you squeeze you into its own mold, but let God remold your minds from within, so that you may prove in practice that the plan of God for you is good, meets all his demands and moves toward the goal of true maturity (Rom. 12:2 Phillips).

Have you allowed God to enter your life and change you inwardly—your values, habits, and even your personality? We're not to see ourselves as stuck with our loathsome traits and weaknesses. God is powerful. His beginning work in us may be small, as a tiny seed or a bit of yeast, but eventually, if we are willing and seek his help, the leaven of his Word grows within us and penetrates every nook and cranny of our being.

### The Treasure in the Field and the Prize Pearl

These two short parables have parallel points and will be considered together.

> The kingdom of heaven is like treasure hidden in a field. When a man found it, he hid it again, and then in his joy went and sold all he had and bought that field (Matt. 13:44).

> Again, the kingdom of heaven is like a merchant looking for fine pearls. When he found one of great value, he went away and sold everything he had and bought it (Matt. 13:45–46).

Oh, the joy of finding a valuable treasure! Isn't that the lesson of both these parables? When the thing of value was found, the finder desired it above all else and gave up all that he had to acquire the prized possession. Did you notice that the treasure in the field was discovered accidentally while the finder was going about his daily work, whereas the merchant found his pearl after a long search?

We can miss the point of these two stories if we let ourselves get sidetracked by such questions as the ethics of the man who purchased the field in which he had secretly reburied the treasure, or the practical wisdom of the merchant who sold everything he owned to buy the exquisite pearl. (What would the impoverished man do with his pearl—just sit and gaze at it?) The purpose of these parables is to highlight the supreme value of discovering the message of the kingdom. Jesus shows that when we are confronted by the good news of his kingdom and see its incomparable value, whether that happens accidentally and unexpectedly, or else after a restless search and comparison of many religions, the joy of our discovery compels us to commit ourselves and all that we have to this new relationship with our King. There are lesser pearls in the world which we can pursue that also bring some measure of satisfaction and joy. These may include intellectual and artistic pursuits, career, travel, public service, etc., but when we realize the eternal significance and value of the pearl that represents the kingdom of God, we see these other pearls to be cheap imitations, like flamboyant costume jewelry compared with a string of elegant, real pearls.

To be a citizen of the kingdom of God means to come under the King's authority, protection, and care. It means having a new relationship with him which causes us to reexamine our goals, ambitions, and habits. What amazes us when we do this is that the gains far outweigh the losses. We give up things that really do not satisfy and gain a more abundant life of peace and joy in Christ Jesus. As Jim Elliott stated so well, "That man is no fool who gives up that which he cannot keep to gain that which he cannot lose."

Are you encouraged by these six parables? Are you rejoicing that God is still at work calling men and women into his kingdom and giving them the privilege of bringing his message of hope and peace to a lost and needy world? Do you appreciate the incomparable worth of this calling? Take the promises, the warnings, and the powerful teachings of these parables and let them permeate your being and raise to a new level your commitment and energy to serve our glorious King.

# 5

## The Parable of the Two Debtors

| Primary Scripture Reading | Supplementary References |
|---|---|
| Luke 7:36–50 | Mark 1:15 |
| | Luke 5:31–32; 15:10 |
| | John 3:14–18 |
| | Acts 16:29–33 |
| | Ephesians 2:8–9 |

### Questions for Study and Discussion

1. Read the interesting episode described in Luke 7:36–50. Why did Simon want to invite Jesus to his house for dinner, do you suppose? (See also Luke 7:29–30.)

   Do you think Simon was open-minded and sincere in wanting to get to know Jesus? Why or why not?

2. What, do you think, was Simon's reasoning behind his remark in verse 39?

3. What did the actions of the sinful woman, presumably a prostitute, reveal about her self-image and her attitude toward Jesus?

4. What significance do you see in the way Simon treated Jesus as his guest (vv. 44–46)? List all the contrasts you see between Simon's and the woman's treatment of Jesus.

5. Jesus asked Simon, "Do you see this woman?" What did Simon see when he looked at her and what did he fail to see that Jesus saw?

6. How did Jesus' parable and explanation (vv. 41–46) answer Simon's thoughts in verse 39?

7. What evidences of true faith did Jesus see that prompted him to make the remarkable statement he made in verse 50?

   What do you consider to be the essential elements of saving faith? (See Mark 1:15; Luke 5:31–32; 15:10; John 3:14–18; Acts 16:29–33; Eph. 2:8–9.)

*T*he parable of the two debtors is rather short with an obvious point, but the way Jesus used it in the fascinating episode that prompted it brings out some of the deepest and most beautiful teaching on love and forgiveness that we have. It is an example of the way Jesus used stories to make his point to a critical audience as well as to teach deep spiritual truth and challenge his listeners to examine their attitudes and their lives.

We understand the episode and parable best if we assume that Jesus had already been teaching and preaching in the town where Simon and the notorious woman lived. We can assume also that the woman had heard Jesus teach and that Simon, if he had not personally heard Jesus, had heard what people were saying about this young itinerant preacher. What happened at Simon's house is an example of the mixed reception Jesus was receiving, as recorded in Luke 7:16–17 and 29–30. Many people, including such despised sinners as tax collectors, had responded to John the Baptist's call for repentance and were open to Jesus' similar call to repentance and faith and to his message that the kingdom of God was at hand (Mark 1:15; Luke 4:43–44). What Jesus taught about true righteousness and forgiveness now made sense to them. Many Pharisees, on the other hand, refused to submit to the baptism of repentance preached by John (Matt. 21:31–32) and also rejected Jesus' message. It seems likely that Simon was one of those who was skeptical about Jesus.

### Simon's Invitation

Simon was apparently a prominent, well-to-do citizen in his town. He possessed a house and means sufficient to allow him to put on a dinner to which his friends and a visitor like Jesus could be invited. Such a dinner would be a prolonged affair with ample time to talk about theological and religious issues. During the dinner, the guests would recline on low couches set up in the courtyard around a low central table on which the food would be placed. They would lie on their left sides, propped up by their left arms, leaving their right arms free to reach the food. Lying at a slight angle to the table with their knees bent, their feet would point away from the table as well as from the guest lying next to them. Sandals would have been removed, and servants could move along the outside of the couches to wash the feet of the guests.

One aspect of their customs that may seem peculiar to us was the lack of privacy. Interested people who were not invited to the dinner could come to watch and listen to the conversation. They would even be allowed to enter the house and to stand or sit along the outside walls.

It's interesting to speculate why Simon invited Jesus to dinner. He apparently wanted to observe Jesus and to test him rather than honor him. Jesus had caused quite a stir in his town, and some people were even calling him a prophet. But Simon remained unconvinced and may have invited Jesus to his house on a "show me" basis. If Simon were to change his opinion and take seriously what Jesus was teaching, Jesus would first have to prove himself. He was, in a sense, putting Jesus on trial and setting himself up as judge.

As the dinner guests arrived, customary etiquette required that the host greet friends who were his social equals by kissing them on both cheeks or, in the case of an esteemed rabbi or nobleman, by kissing his hand. The host would also arrange for his guests to remove their sandals and have his servants wash their dusty feet. Often he would pour a little scented oil on the guests' heads (Ps. 23:5). Simon's failure to honor Jesus with any of these usual courtesies seems to indicate contempt for his guest and perhaps his intention to insult him publicly.

### An Interruption

One of the uninvited observers standing along the wall was a woman of bad reputation, probably a prostitute. She had undoubtedly heard Jesus teach and had responded to his message. Hearing that Simon had invited Jesus to his house and longing to be near him to hear more of his teaching, she may have thought to herself, "Do I dare to go to the house of this important Pharisee? If they recognize me, will I be thrown out?" But Jesus had given her so much joy and hope that she didn't care what might happen to her. She would go no matter what, and she would take with her a beautiful jar of expensive perfume, probably a prized possession.

The woman apparently arrived at Simon's house before Jesus did (Luke 7:45). We are not told how long she stood there waiting, or if Simon recognized her when she came in. Our first picture of her is her standing at Jesus' feet weeping. Why was she crying? Perhaps her tears were those of repentance for her former lifestyle. Perhaps they were tears of joy because she felt forgiven and clean for the first time in her adult life. It is also possible that she was crying because of the cruel, insulting treatment given to Jesus by Simon. Whatever the case, she was overcome with emotion as she came forward to be near Jesus.

Notice the humility of the woman. She did not presume to touch or kiss Jesus' face or even his hand. Instead, she stood or knelt at his feet. Because she was weeping uncontrollably, her tears fell on Jesus' unwashed, dusty feet. She hadn't expected to be so overcome with emotion, for she had brought along nothing with which to wipe away her tears. Impulsively, she let down her hair and wiped Jesus' feet with her tresses. Then she kissed his feet over and over and lovingly poured her expensive perfume on them. Think of how shocking her actions must have been to Simon and his guests. I imagine that all conversation ceased, everyone stopped eating, and all heads turned to watch this unexpected drama. To make matters worse, Jewish women were not supposed to let down their hair in public. That was thought to be an indecent, intimate act and, according to the Talmud, was considered grounds for divorce if done in public (Kenneth Bailey, *Through Peasant Eyes*, Eerdmans [Grand Rapids: 1980], 1–21). But this humble woman cared little what Simon and his friends thought, so determined was she to express her great love and devotion to Jesus. She literally worshiped him. With her impulsive actions she honored Jesus in all the ways Simon had failed to honor him.

### Simon's Interpretation

Simon, startled by what he had just witnessed, watched to see how Jesus would handle this intrusion. This may have been what he was waiting for. He recognized the woman and knew her background and sordid profession. He thought to himself, "If this man were a prophet, he would know who is touching him and what kind of woman she is—that she is a sinner." If Jesus didn't rebuff her and tell her to get lost, then surely he must have no special God-given powers or insights.

But Jesus did not push the woman away. Instead, he accepted her devotion and worship. As for Simon, he had seen enough. He thought he had his answer: This man is no prophet! His purpose in putting on the dinner was satisfied. But Simon didn't know how wrong he was and how far his interpretation was off the mark. Simon, like the Pharisees described in Matthew 9:10–13 and Luke 15:1–2, didn't understand that Jesus' ministry was to lost sinners and that even the worst offenders were invited to repent, to believe, to be forgiven, and to enter the kingdom of heaven. Jesus did indeed know the woman. He knew her heart. He saw her humility and the depth of her repentance, which was something Simon could not fathom. Simon saw her only as the sinful woman she had been. He did not take much stock in repentance. What was important to him was to keep all the rituals and customs of his religious traditions, and he thought he was doing a pretty good job of it, thank you. So for what should he repent? But he was due for yet another shock.

## Jesus' Interpretation

So far, not a word had been spoken aloud since the woman came forward and knelt at Jesus' feet. It was Jesus who broke the silence when he turned to his host and said, "Simon, I have something to tell you." He then proceeded to relate a short parable.

> Two men owed money to a certain moneylender. One owed him five hundred denarii, and the other fifty. Neither of them had the money to pay him back, so he canceled the debts of both (Luke 7:41–42).

To appreciate this story we must assume that both borrowers were in dire financial straits and that neither had any way to repay his debt. Also, because a denarius was equal to a typical day's pay at that time (Matt. 20:1–2), the larger debt was equivalent to nearly two year's wages, about the size of a typical mortgage, while the smaller debt was equal to about two month's pay. Debtors could be thrown in jail in those days, so defaulting on a loan was a serious matter for a borrower. Jesus' story, however, had a surprise ending. The moneylender graciously and unexpectedly forgave both debts.

As Jesus finished his story, he looked at Simon and asked, "Now which of them will love him more?" Simon was probably uneasy about being drawn into answering so obvious a question and, because he did not know the point Jesus was going to make, answered cautiously, "I suppose the one who had the bigger debt canceled."

After he drew from Simon the only possible answer to his question, Jesus proceeded to use the story to interpret what had just happened in the scene involving the woman. What he said next was another surprise in what had turned out to be a very surprising evening. Guests just did not complain to their hosts in that culture, regardless of the quality of the treatment they received. But I think Jesus knew that only the most blunt and drastic measures would provide any hope of penetrating the hardened mind of this Pharisee and bring about changes. So he looked at the woman and said to Simon, "Do you see this woman?" Dumb question, or was it? Of course Simon saw her, but only externally. To him she was still a despised harlot. He didn't see her changed heart as Jesus did. He didn't understand the significance of her actions, nor did he appreciate the sincerity of her repentance or the possibility of her being forgiven. To Simon, acceptance by God could not be gained that easily; it had to be earned by scrupulously keeping the law. But Jesus, knowing both her heart and Simon's, saw in them a tremendous contrast, which he then exposed by comparing their actions.

> I came to your house. You did not give me any water for my feet, but she wet my feet with her tears and wiped them with her hair. You did not give me a kiss, but this woman, from the time I entered, has not stopped kissing my feet. You did not put oil on my head, but she has poured perfume on my feet. Therefore, I tell you, her many sins have been forgiven—for she loved much. But he who has been forgiven little loves little (Luke 7:44–48).

The woman did all the loving things Simon had deliberately neglected to do. Simon had not shown Jesus even the minimum respect and honor any guest has a right to expect from his host. In three respects—a kiss of welcome, foot washing, and anointing—he had failed, while the woman, who was not even the host, had done them all with obvious sincerity. "Therefore," Jesus said, referring back to the parable, "her many sins have been forgiven— for she loved much" (v. 47 NIV). Did Jesus mean to say that this woman earned forgiveness *because* she loved much? It appears that Jesus' statement could just as well be translated, "Her many sins have been forgiven, therefore she loved much." The New English Bible gives this sense to its rendering, which reads, "Her great love proves that her many sins have been forgiven." This understanding of Jesus' statement is also consistent with the parable to which it refers. Clearly, the lender's reason for forgiving the debts was not that he first saw how much the debtors loved him.

Although the main point of the parable concerns the response to having one's debts forgiven, there is another observation about the act of forgiveness that we can draw from Jesus' story. What happens when a lender forgives debts? Who pays for them? There is no such thing as just forgetting about debts. Any forgiven debt decreases the assets (accounts receivable) of the lender, so he literally pays them himself if he cancels them. In applying the parable, Jesus equates the forgiveness of debt to the forgiveness of sin and gives us a picture of the way God forgives us. We are all spiritual debtors in God's sight—paupers who have no assets of any value. Some may seem to owe more than others, at least by our human scale of reckoning, but none of us can pay what we owe. So God mercifully pays the debt for our sins himself when he forgives us on the basis of our repentance and faith, and we can claim this forgiveness or canceling of our debt through faith in him. Paul explains God's gracious actions on our behalf this way:

> But now a righteousness from God, apart from the law, has been made known, to which the Law and the Prophets testify. This righteousness from God comes through faith in Jesus Christ to all who believe. There is no difference, for all have sinned and fall short of the glory of God, and are justified freely by his grace through the redemption that came by Christ Jesus. God presented him as a sacrifice of atonement, through faith in his blood (Rom. 3:21–25).

What a beautiful picture of repentance and of forgiveness and justification through faith in Christ Jesus this episode presents. The woman's actions showed that she realized what had happened to her was a result of pure grace. But what about Simon? After Jesus said, "I tell you, her many sins have been forgiven—for she loved much," which clearly referred to the woman, he added, "But he who has been forgiven little loves little." Did that refer to Simon? How much did he love? Did he love at all? Perhaps not. His thoughts and actions showed only contempt and rejection of Jesus. But if he didn't love at all, was he forgiven at all? That was the burning question Jesus left with Simon. The parable was Jesus' loving call to Simon to look at his own heart as well as to reconsider his judgment of the woman. Here again Jesus uses a parable to challenge people then and now to put themselves into his story and to examine their lives and their relationship to God.

Do you identify more with the woman in this episode or with Simon? If you were brought up in a strong Christian home, as I was, perhaps your situation and lifestyle are really more like Simon's, and you are subject to his tendencies and attitudes. Perhaps your life has been rather sheltered because of an advantageous environment which made it easy to live a typically "Christian" lifestyle. You may even have been envious at times of the dramatic testimonies of those believers who were saved from more blatantly sinful situations. If this is your experience, the danger you face is that, like Simon, your lack of participation in the godless, promiscuous lifestyles of this generation can make you less aware of what God has done for you and less thankful.

We forget that our debt to God includes what we have been protected from as well as forgiveness for the secret sins of lust, envy, jealousy, covetousness that we all have. These weaknesses that we don't like to face up to and try to keep hidden would, no doubt, have led us into more heinous and overt sins if our circumstances had been different. How thankful we should be that we have been spared the heartaches and the very real emotional and physical scars of a degraded life. Our love and appreciation for God's grace should be just as sincere and fervent as that of the forgiven prostitute, if not more.

In his challenge to Simon, Jesus put his finger on the basic problem of self-righteousness and why it desensitizes the heart and is so deadly to the spirit. It's easy to fall into the trap of thinking we are obeying God's will for our lives and somehow merit his love and acceptance more than some others with whom we compare ourselves. Simon's actions demonstrated pride, lack of love, judgmental spirit, and lack of sensitivity, but he wasn't aware of it. Doesn't Simon's view of himself and his judgmental attitude toward the repentant woman remind you of the older brother in the parable of the prodigal son (Luke 15)? He objected to his father's acceptance of his repentant, wayward brother. Isn't Simon also like the Pharisee who went to the temple to pray, whom Jesus contrasted with a tax collector standing nearby? About the Pharisee Jesus said:

> The Pharisee stood up and prayed about himself: "God, I thank you that I am not like other men—robbers, evildoers, adulterers—or even like this tax collector. I fast twice a week and give a tenth of all I get" (Luke 18:11–12).

The woman's view of herself was like that of the humble tax collector, about whom Jesus said:

> The tax collector stood at a distance. He would not even look up to heaven, but beat his breast and said, "God, have mercy on me, a sinner." I tell you that this man, rather than the other, went home justified before God. For everyone who exalts himself will be humbled, and he who humbles himself will be exalted (Luke 18:13–14).

Simon did not see himself as Paul did, who referred to himself as the worst of sinners. Paul wrote:

Here is a trustworthy saying that deserves full acceptance: Christ Jesus came into the world to save sinners—of whom I am the worst. But for that very reason I was shown mercy so that in me, the worst of sinners, Christ Jesus might display his unlimited patience as an example for those who would believe on him and receive eternal life (1 Tim. 1:15–16).

Paul's experience and self-image seem so much like that of the woman in Luke 7 that I can imagine her going up to Paul in heaven, embracing him, and thanking him for expressing her feelings exactly. Both of them had a deep love for the Lord because they were aware of the depth of their sin and felt the joy of being forgiven. Such love can also be ours if we lay out before the Lord the ways we have failed him, both in things we have done and have not done, and ask his forgiveness. The more we are aware of God's holiness and our unworthiness, the more real his grace becomes and the more overwhelmed we will be by his love and forgiveness.

### Final Instructions

Jesus made two final comments to the woman. With great authority he said, "Your sins are forgiven." Can you imagine how much that broken, contrite woman needed to hear those reassuring words? I'm sure she never forgot them as long as she lived. I like to think that she reminded herself of them over and over to strengthen her resolve as she began to lead her new life. Then Jesus added, "Your faith has saved you; go in peace." She was heartbroken over her sins, had brought them to Jesus, and trusted him for forgiveness. Her love and honor for Jesus overflowed, and now she worshiped him as her Lord. Repentance and faith, so often mentioned in Scripture as requirements for salvation (Mark 1:15; Luke 5:31–32; 15:10; John 3:14–18; Acts 16:29–33; Eph. 2:8–9), were clearly evident in this lost sinner who was found.

When Jesus said to the woman, "Your sins are forgiven," Simon's guests realized the implications of the statement and said to one another, "Who is this who even forgives sins?" (Luke 7:48–9). Earlier, when Jesus was about to heal the paralytic (Mark 2:5–7), he made a similar statement: "Son, your sins are forgiven." The scribes who were present were incensed when they heard that. They said, "Why does this fellow talk like that? He's blaspheming! Who can forgive sins but God alone?" This same question now confronted Simon and his friends. Who did this man think he was, claiming to do what only God can do? Either Jesus was a special representative of God or he was an outrageous blasphemer. Not only his words but also his actions in Simon's house constituted a strong claim for deity. By accepting the adulation and worship of the forgiven woman, Jesus claimed to be worthy of it as well as responsible for what had happened to her. The harlot invited Jesus into her life and allowed him to clean house and change everything. Simon, on the other hand, invited Jesus into his house but had no intention of changing his life. Jesus' presence had no effect on him, whereas the woman became a new creation in Christ, her old life was gone, her new life had begun (2 Cor. 5:17).

We who study this episode are also confronted by the person of Jesus. If we have responded to Jesus' call to repent and believe, as the woman did, do other people see our great joy and gratitude for having been forgiven, and does that draw them to our Lord? As forgiven sinners, are we lovers of God? Do we share Jesus' love and acceptance of the outcast sinners of our society? Do we love much or do we love little?

# 6

## The Parable of the Good Samaritan

| Primary Scripture Reading | Supplementary References |
| --- | --- |
| Luke 10:25–37 | Numbers 19:11–16 |
| | Ezra 4:1–5 |
| | Nehemiah 4:1–19 |
| | Matthew 5:17–20; 20:34; |
| |   23:1–7, 23–28 |
| | Luke 7:13; 9:51–56; 10:33; |
| |   15:20; 17:11–19; 18:18–30 |
| | John 3:1–16; 4:1–42; 8:48 |

### Questions for Study and Discussion

1. Read through the parable: Luke 10:25–37. In what way, in your opinion, did the expert in the law try to test Jesus with his first question (v. 25)?


   Why was Jesus' conversation with this expert so different from his discussion with another expert in John 3:1–16?


   Based on Jesus' answer in Luke 10:28 and his statement in Matthew 5:17–20, what was his attitude toward the law?

91

2. In his second question, "And who is my neighbor?" what typical attitude did the lawyer reveal, and what kind of answer was he looking for, do you suppose? (See Matt. 23:1–7, 23–28.)

3. List all the reasons you can, religious and practical, why the priest and the Levite would not want to stop to help a half-dead traveler. (See Num. 19:11–16.)

   Give an example from your experience when you failed to take time to help someone in need and regretted it later.

4. After reading the following passages, describe the relationship between the Jews and the Samaritans: Ezra 4:1–5; Nehemiah 4:1–6; Luke 9:51–56; 17:11–19; John 4:1–10, 27, 39–42; 8:48.

   From these verses, what was Jesus' attitude toward the Samaritans?

5. Enumerate the kind and generous things the Samaritan did for the robbery victim. Estimate the out-of-pocket cost, at today's prices, and the amount of time the Samaritan spent taking care of the needy stranger.

6. Read Luke 10:33; 7:13; 15:20; Matthew 20:34 and describe the emotion expressed in each situation and the result of this feeling. (The same Greek word to express feelings or emotion is used in all four verses.)

How can we test the depth of our compassion for people in need of help?

7. Why did Jesus refuse to define explicitly for the lawyer who was his neighbor, do you think?

In what way did Jesus' parable change the focus of the question asked in Luke 10:29?

Whom do you consider to be your neighbor?

Describe what it would mean for you if you truly loved your neighbor as yourself.

8. Did Jesus' answer in Luke 10:28 imply that the lawyer could gain eternal life by keeping the law? Why or why not?

*H*ave you ever talked when you should have listened? Have you ever asked a question and been sorry later that you asked it? Or have you ever decided too late that you asked the wrong question? It happens, doesn't it? It happened one day as Jesus was teaching his followers. Here is Luke's account of how the incident began:

On one occasion an expert in the law stood up to test Jesus. "Teacher," he asked, "what must I do to inherit eternal life?"

"What is written in the Law?" he replied. "How do you read it?" He answered: "'Love the Lord your God with all your heart and with all your soul and with all your strength and with all your mind'; and, 'Love your neighbor as yourself.'" "You have answered correctly," Jesus replied. "Do this and you will live." But he wanted to justify himself, so he asked Jesus, "And who is my neighbor?" (Luke 10:25–29).

### The First Question

Picture the scene. Jesus was apparently teaching a group of people seated around him. We are not told where this took place, whether outside on a hillside or inside a synagogue. Wherever it was, an expert in Jewish religious law who was present among the listeners stood up and asked, "Teacher, what must I do to inherit eternal life?" Good question! But wait a minute, something doesn't add up. Here was a trained expert in the law asking Jesus, an untrained layman, a very basic question about religion. Was he really that humble? Was he trying to learn something new from a teacher he respected? No way! He asked his question to test Jesus. He undoubtedly had his own answer clearly in mind and most likely intended to use Jesus' words against him in some way. Did you catch the legalistic bent in his question? He asked, "What must *I* do?" rather than "What has *God* done for me?"

The lawyer may have been an expert in the law, but Jesus was an expert at detecting and exposing insincerity. Notice how Jesus turned the question back to his questioner: "What is written in the Law? How do you read it?" The scribe answered: "Love the Lord your God with all your heart and with all your soul and with all your strength and with all your mind, and love your neighbor as yourself." This was another good answer—impeccable. It was a well-known summary of two Old Testament verses, Deuteronomy 6:5 and Leviticus 19:18, and Jesus himself had recited this in Matthew 22:34–40 and in Mark 12:28–31. The Pharisees probably carried these very verses in little leather packets, called phylacteries, that they bound to their left wrists and foreheads to show that God's law was close to their hearts and minds (Deut. 6:4–9).

Now it was Jesus' turn to respond, and he sent the ball back into the lawyer's court. He said, "You have answered correctly. Do this and you will live." I don't know if that response surprised the lawyer, but it may surprise us. Why would Jesus say that? Did Jesus tell this man that he could be saved by keeping the law rather than by repentance for failure to keep the law and faith in the atoning sacrifice of God's Lamb? If so, wouldn't that be salvation by works and a contradiction of such passages as Romans 3:19–20 and Ephesians 2:8–9? Well now, let's think about that. Perhaps Jesus intended to lead the lawyer to see what it would mean to be accepted by God on the basis of the law, what it would mean to keep the law perfectly, and what it would mean to love God with his total being at all times and to love others just as much as himself, with no limits. The apostle Paul, a Pharisee himself (Acts 23:6), recognized that his human nature made it impossible for him to keep the law, even if he wanted to. He said, "We know that the law is spiritual, but I am unspiritual, sold as a slave to sin. . . . For I have the desire to do what is good, but I cannot carry it out" (Rom. 7:14, 18). If the lawyer had looked at himself as honestly as Paul did, he would have stopped right there and uttered the same prayer as the humble tax collector in Luke 18:13: "God, have mercy on me, a sinner." It's hard, isn't it, for us to come to the place where we are truly honest with ourselves about our sinfulness. Until we do, we will fail, as did this lawyer, to see our false pride and self-righteousness and will instead go right on asking the wrong questions and pursuing the wrong answers.

## The Second Question

The lawyer, if he had been smart, would have sat down at this point and listened. But no, he "wanted to justify himself" and so asked yet another question. It's unclear from the text in what way or before whom he wanted to justify himself. As an expert in discussing questions of the law, he may have been embarrassed that Jesus had deftly made him answer his own question and had not been drawn into a public debate on technicalities of religious law. Or, as a Pharisee and keeper of the Torah, he may have thought that there would obviously be no question about his keeping the first part of the commandment: to love God. After all, religious duties filled his life. On the other hand, there might be some question about how well he kept the corollary law: "Love your neighbor as yourself." He was more vulnerable there. There were a few people he didn't get along with, and some who didn't like him. The quality of his relationships with others was something that could be observed and judged. Whatever his reason, he decided this was where he would draw Jesus into making a definition or list with which he could argue. As a scribe, he had memorized all the comments of previous generations of experts on the subject of neighbors and how to show love to them. He could talk endlessly about different points of view and contingencies. In his mind, nothing that pertained to keeping God's law should be left undefined and open-ended, and so he asked Jesus, "And who is my neighbor?"

What answer did the lawyer expect? Based on Leviticus 19:18, a view that was widely held among the Jews was: "Love your neighbor, the Israelite." We also know from their actions and statements recorded in the Gospels that the Pharisees restricted the definition of neighbor even further to those they considered spiritually deserving: other practising Pharisees (Matt. 9:10–11; John 7:47–49).

The crowd must have waited eagerly for Jesus' answer, for many of them felt accepted by Jesus in a way they never had been accepted by the Pharisees. Also, they knew the Pharisees had strongly criticized Jesus for associating with "tax collectors and sinners" and outcasts of society. As before, Jesus artfully dodged being drawn into a long legalistic discussion. He did not answer the question directly; instead, he told a story that has become one of the best-known parables of all time—a story that would again force the lawyer to answer his own question.

### The Parable

In reply Jesus said: "A man was going down from Jerusalem to Jericho, when he fell into the hands of robbers. They stripped him of his clothes, beat him and went away, leaving him half dead. A priest happened to be going down the same road, and when he saw the man, he passed by on the other side. So too, a Levite, when he came to the place and saw him, passed by on the other side. But a Samaritan, as he traveled, came where the man was; and when he saw him, he took pity on him. He went to him and bandaged his wounds, pouring on oil and wine. Then he put the man on his own donkey, took him to an inn and took care of him. The next day he took out two silver coins and gave them to the innkeeper. 'Look after him,' he said, 'and when I return, I will reimburse you for any extra expense you may have.' Which of these three do you think was a neighbor to the man who fell into the hands of robbers?" The expert in the law replied, "The one who had mercy on him." Jesus told him, "Go and do likewise" (Luke 10:30–37).

In his first two sentences, Jesus laid out the setting for the story before he introduced the three characters one by one. He certainly chose the right spot for his episode. I traveled this road by tour bus a few years ago and observed the desolate, hilly wilderness through which it passes. The road is steep and winding, dropping over three thousand feet in the seventeen miles between Jerusalem and Jericho. It was not hard to imagine that this wild country would have provided excellent cover for roving bands of brigands in Jesus' day. It would have been a dangerous road to travel without protection. Nevertheless, it was a much-traveled road at the time because it was a trade route and because many of the Jews liked to live in, or at least visit, the warmer, lush Jordan valley about twelve hundred feet below sea level.

The first traveler to come on the unfortunate, half-dead man was a priest traveling from Jerusalem to Jericho. His direction of travel is significant, for it means that he was not going to Jerusalem to serve his stint in the temple.[1] If he had been, he might have had a legitimate excuse not to touch a prone body. According to Jewish law, if he touched a dead body, he could not have served in the temple until he had gone through the rites of purification, a process that lasted a week (Num. 19:11–16). Furthermore, even if the victim were still alive, how could he tell if the poor fellow was a Jew and deserving of his help? The man had been stripped of all identifying clothing. Why, he might be a sinner, one of those despicable collaborating tax collectors, or even a Gentile! There were just too many questions and he was too busy to get involved. Besides, it really wasn't his problem. The government should do a better job of patrolling this road. It was their fault. He would register a complaint the next time he was in Jerusalem. This resolve made him feel better, so he passed by on the other side of the road.

Next came a Levite, also a cleric but of lower standing. Levites assisted priests in the temple. From the standpoint

---

[1]For a glimpse of how the priestly system worked, see Luke 1:8–9, 23, which describes when Zechariah was chosen by lot to take his turn to serve as priest in the temple.

of ceremonial purity, he had less reason than the priest not to give aid, but he did not stop, either. Note the nearly identical wording used to describe the actions of the two clerics. They came to the place, they saw the helpless man, and they passed by on the other side. The implication seems to be that they used their involvement in the Lord's work to excuse their indifference to the one in need. However, by doing this they ignored God's warning given through Hosea and repeated by Jesus in Matthew 9:13: "I desire mercy, not sacrifice."

Jesus' listeners probably enjoyed the way he showed up the weaknesses of the clergy. As lay people, they may have thought, "Amen! Give it to 'em. Lay it on those pious religious types." Now they were all ears, wondering what would happen next. Who would rescue the wounded traveler? Would it be one of them—a Jewish layman, the next lower rank in their religious hierarchy? They were probably shocked out of their wits when the hero turned out to be, of all people, a Samaritan!

It must have seemed to the people of that day that Jews and Samaritans had always hated each other. Indeed, the root of the problem dated back more than seven hundred years when the conquering Assyrians deported most of the Israelites from the northern kingdom and replaced them with people from several other countries. It is thought they did this to diffuse nationalistic feelings and reduce the likelihood of revolt. As a result, the people of Samaria were of mixed origin and developed a religion that was a mixture of Judaism and paganism. Actual hostilities between the Jews and Samaritans erupted when Jews from the southern kingdom who had been exiled to Babylon were allowed to return to Jerusalem beginning about 530 B.C. They were led successively by Zerubbabel, Ezra, and Nehemiah, and began to rebuild the temple and the walls of Jerusalem. The returning Jews, determined to maintain the purity of their religion, refused to let the semipagan Samaritans participate in the rebuilding of the temple and in worship there. As a result, the Samaritans tried in every possible way to hinder and stop the rebuilding (Ezra 4:1–5; Neh. 4:1–6).

The animosity between the two groups was still very much alive in Jesus' day. John wrote in his Gospel that "Jews do not associate with Samaritans" (John 4:9). When Jews traveled between Galilee and Jerusalem, they went out of their way to avoid passing through Samaria. The Samaritans also did their part to fan the flames. Josephus mentions in his *Antiquities* (18:II, 2) that the Samaritans infuriated the Jews by desecrating their temple during Passover by sneaking in at night and littering it with dead bodies and bones. Even Jesus got caught in this messy situation when he and his disciples were refused lodging in a Samaritan village. The disciples got so angry at this affront that they wanted Jesus to call down fire from heaven to wipe out that town (Luke 9:51–56). At another time, the Pharisees hurled this accusation at Jesus (John 8:48): "Aren't we right in saying that you are a Samaritan and demon-possessed?" This was the worst insult they could think of. Jesus, however, showed no trace of this prejudice against the Samaritans. John in his Gospel records that Jesus insisted on walking through Samaria, spoke to the woman at Jacob's well, and remained for several days in her village to teach the new believers (John 4). That must have been a real eye-opening experience for the disciples.

Jesus introduced the Samaritan into his story in a very matter-of-fact way, using almost the same words he had used for the Jewish clerics: "But a Samaritan, as he traveled, came where the man was; and when he saw him . . . " (Luke 10:33). There the similarity ended, for this time the one who came upon the injured traveler took pity on him and did everything possible to help him. The Samaritan was the hero. What a bombshell!

The Greek word *esplanchnisthé* translated "took pity" in verse 33 (NIV) may also be translated "had compassion" or "heart went out." Luke used the same word to describe the father's reaction when he saw his prodigal son coming home (Luke 15:20), and again to characterize Jesus' feeling when he met the widow at Nain whose only son had died and was about to be buried (Luke 7:13). It denotes a deep compassionate feeling that churns up one's insides and leads to action. Notice how the Samaritan demonstrated his deep feeling of pity for the helpless victim. He first applied what home remedies he knew as first aid: wine to disinfect and purify, oil to soothe, and bandages to staunch the flow of blood and protect the wounds from dust and dirt. He then went further; he sat or laid the stranger on his own mount and, walking alongside as a servant, took him to an inn where he cared for him for the rest of that day and night. The next day the Samaritan paid the innkeeper for their lodging and gave him additional money to care for the wounded man until he was well enough to leave under his own power. He also promised that, if it took longer than expected for the man to recover, he would be back to pay the additional cost. His kindness left no stone unturned.

What an amazing story for a Jew to tell a Jewish crowd! An uncomfortable hush must have settled over them as they waited to hear what would happen next. Jesus looked straight at the lawyer and asked, "Which of these three do you think was a neighbor to the man who fell into the hands of robbers?" (Luke 10:36). There was only one possible answer, of course, and the lawyer was stuck with it. He mumbled a reply, avoiding the hated S-word: "The one who had mercy on him." Jesus, speaking with the unashamed authority that was rightfully his as the incarnate Lord, then said to the expert in the law: "Go and do likewise."

Ponder for a moment what Jesus accomplished with this powerful story he told in answer to the lawyer's question. He demonstrated that to maintain religious purity at the expense of showing mercy does not fulfill the law of love. No one is too holy to get his or her hands dirty helping those who need it. He also showed that anyone who truly loves others as himself would not even bother to ask, "Who is my neighbor?" That was the wrong question. And he forced the lawyer to face up to the much more important question, What does it mean to love your neighbor as yourself? Through this unforgettable episode, Jesus pictured the kind of love it takes to obey God's command. In effect, he told the lawyer, "All right, you want to gain eternal life by keeping the law? Well, this is what it means to love your neighbor as yourself: When you find someone who needs your help, you are to love and care for that one, even if he or she is a stranger, a member of another race, or your most despised enemy." Does that seem difficult or impossible? Remember, this is the easy half of the summary of the law; the other half commands us to love God, whom we cannot see and can scarcely imagine, with our total being—heart, soul, strength, and mind.

None of us can fully understand what it means to love Almighty God with all that we are and all that we have. That is far beyond our comprehension, not to mention our ability. On the other hand, this parable gives us clear insight into what it means to obey the other part of the commandment—love your neighbor as yourself—which relates to our relationships within the physical world in which we live. When we see the picture as Jesus presented it, we, along with Jesus' audience, will realize how far short we fall of keeping God's holy law. Jesus has shown us a standard of love that makes us hang our heads in shame.

Christianity, however, is a religion of grace. That's the good news of the gospel! None of us can keep God's law perfectly. In fact it is "through the law we become conscious of sin" (Rom. 3:20). Until we are convicted and silenced before the law, we cannot even hear the gospel. But if we humbly repent, realizing that "the wages of sin is death," we can look to God for mercy and accept his promise that "the gift of God is eternal life in Christ Jesus our Lord" (Rom. 6:23).

If we have accepted by faith Jesus' sacrificial death as the atonement for our sins, we are overwhelmed by God's love and grace in forgiving us and adopting us as his children. From this gratitude flows a desire to please him, obey him, and live as he wants us to live. Loving our neighbors then follows naturally, for the more we understand and appreciate what God has done for us, the more our relationships with other people will be characterized by the kind of love exhibited by God for us—the kind Jesus illustrated for us in this story and the kind he demonstrated in his life. There can be no limit to our definition of neighbor, and no separation of our love for God from our love for God's creatures. Like the priest and the Levite in Jesus' parable, we can be so busy because of the schedules we set up for our religious life and church affairs that we don't have time to notice and help those in need around us. If we have allowed ourselves to fall into this trap, then our priorities are out of kilter. Our agendas must be interruptible; we must have our eyes open for the unplanned opportunities God sends for us to demonstrate his love, just as the Samaritan did in Jesus' parable.

Pray that God will touch and open your *soul* so you can fathom his great love for you through Christ our Savior. Pray that he will stir and soften your *heart* so you will be sensitive to and have compassion for the needs of others. Pray that he will quicken your *mind* so you may be wise in providing needed help and care, and pray for *strength* to be able to act on your compassion. To the extent you do these things you demonstrate with your whole being your gratitude and love to God for the abundant life he has given you in Christ Jesus.

# 7

## The Parable of the Rich Fool

**Primary Scripture Reading**

Luke 12:1–21

**Supplementary References**

Exodus 20:1–17
Luke 5:29; 15:22–24
Colossians 3:5

### Questions for Study and Discussion

1. Read Luke 12:1–21. To whom was Jesus talking and what was he talking about when he was interrupted by the voice from the crowd?

   Why did the young man approach Jesus with his problem, do you think, and what does his interruption indicate to you about him?

2. What implications do you see in Jesus' question to the young man in verse 14, and why did he answer him in this way, do you suppose?

3. Which of the Ten Commandments (Exodus 20) corresponds to Jesus' warning in verse 15, and what is so bad about this sin? (See Col. 3:5.)

4. When faced with the problem of what to do with his bumper crop, how did the rich man arrive at his decision?

   How did the rich man's reaction to his good fortune differ from the reactions described in Luke 5:29 and 15:22–24, and what do their reactions indicate to you about each of these men?

5. God gave the rich man the bumper crop, so why was God displeased with the man's decision to build barns to store it, do you think?

   What other options and factors could the rich man have considered?

6. What does Jesus' phrase "rich toward God" mean to you?

   How does Jesus' warning in Luke 12:21 relate to verse 15?

   What activities or material things in your life hinder you from being "rich toward God"?

7. What actions and attitudes toward possessions and material blessings would you like to change in yourself as a result of what Jesus taught you through this parable?

Show me, O LORD, my life's end and the number of my days;
let me know how fleeting is my life. You have made my
days a mere handbreadth; the span of my years is as nothing before you. Each man's life is but a breath. Man is a mere
phantom as he goes to and fro: He bustles about, but only
in vain; he heaps up wealth, not knowing who will get it
(Ps. 39:4–6).

orry can be debilitating. The problems we
worry about can so consume our minds
that we become unaware of our surround-
ings and are unable to concentrate on anything else. Have
you ever found yourself in that situation? Has your mind
ever been so preoccupied that you couldn't remember what
you had just read or heard? Have you ever found it just
about impossible to listen to a sermon because your
thoughts kept going back to some knotty problem that
bothered you at the time? Most of us have found ourselves
in such situations, perhaps many times. Regardless of the
importance of the subject or the quality of the message we
were hearing, our problem blocked all else from our minds.

There was a young man in Jesus' audience on one particular day who must have found it hard to listen to Jesus,
because his mind was preoccupied. He was worried that
he might not get his share of the family inheritance from
his brother. Jesus had been talking to his disciples in the
presence of a large crowd about such heavy topics as
hypocrisy, the power of Satan, the quality of God's love,
blasphemy of the Holy Spirit, and how to deal with persecution—all fascinating and important subjects—but the
young man was unable to listen. He couldn't get his mind
off his problem. Finally he could stand it no longer. Ignor-

ing the disciples and listening crowd as well as the significance of what Jesus was teaching, he decided to interrupt and demand help from Jesus. Luke gives the account of what happens.

### A Voice from the Crowd

> Meanwhile, when a crowd of many thousands had gathered, so that they were trampling on one another, Jesus began to speak first to his disciples. . . . Someone in the crowd said to him, "Teacher, tell my brother to divide the inheritance with me." Jesus replied, "Man, who appointed me a judge or an arbiter between you?" Then he said to them, "Watch out! Be on your guard against all kinds of greed; a man's life does not consist in the abundance of his possessions" (Luke 12:1, 13–15).

What a rude interruption! How self-centered! It wasn't a polite request for help, it was a demand—a demand for Jesus to take his side in a family dispute. Notice all that the young man assumed when he made his demand: First, that he was right and his brother wrong; second, that his problem was so significant that he was justified in interrupting Jesus; and third, that Jesus would agree with him that he was being treated unfairly and would be willing to help him.

The young gentleman had apparently heard that Jesus was a great teacher and must have presumed that he was a practicing rabbi. Rabbis were expected to apply Jewish religious law to all aspects of Jewish social and religious life and to arbitrate and settle disputes. But Jesus was not a rabbi in the usual sense and was frequently at odds with the way the rabbis interpreted and applied the law. He was in truth much more than a rabbi; he was able to respond to the man's situation by looking into his heart, getting to the root cause of the difficulty, and applying the standard of God's perfect law to expose the young man's real problem.

We are told nothing of the circumstances that caused the disagreement between the brothers, but it's not hard to imagine what may have happened. The father of the two brothers must have died and left his possessions to his sons. According to Mosaic law (Deut. 21:17), the oldest son was to receive a double share of the inheritance and the other sons a single share. In the case of two brothers, the divisions would be two thirds and one third. The father may have thought the brothers would continue to work together harmoniously in the family business or on the family farm, but that didn't happen. As is often the case, friction developed, and apparently one of the sons, most likely the younger, wanted to get out of the joint arrangement, take his share of the inheritance, and strike out on his own. Does that situation sound familiar? It brings to mind the prodigal son, doesn't it?

The problem may have been more complicated than the young man made it sound. There may have been good reasons why the older son was not able to give his brother his share in cash. He may have faced a tough choice: whether to liquidate some of the family property in order to raise the needed cash to pay his brother, or else, if he wanted to keep the family business or farm intact, to try to borrow the funds to pay off his brother. Whatever the difficulty, the brother who appealed to Jesus wanted action and wanted it now.

As the demand was shouted, can't you see all the heads turn first to the young man and then back to Jesus to see what he would do? But Jesus refused to be drawn into this family dispute. His reply was cool and impersonal: "Man, who appointed me a judge or an arbiter between you?" Isn't that a surprising reply for Jesus to make? Didn't he usually make it a priority to help the downtrodden and oppressed? Didn't he go out of his way to heal the blind and the outcast lepers, to befriend the hated tax collectors, and even to defend the woman caught in adultery? But now he rejected flatly a request for help from someone who felt he had been wronged. Why? From his subsequent comments we can infer that Jesus perceived and was concerned about a deeper problem. He knew what lay at the heart of the dispute and apparently wanted to shake up the man and make him face it. The young brother needed a new perspective, and Jesus proceeded to give him one.

### The First Warning (Luke 12:15)

Jesus immediately got down to basics. He said, "Watch out! Be on your guard against all kinds of greed; a man's life does not consist in the abundance of his possessions." Notice how skillfully Jesus wove two elements into this statement. The first was a warning, and the second presented a new way of looking at things. The young man needed to be cautioned about greed, but he also needed a positive principle by which to live and to determine what was important in life. What Jesus told him applied not only to his present situation but to his future choices as well.

Jesus' answer restated the last of the Ten Commandments, which reads: "You shall not covet . . . anything that belongs to your neighbor" (Exod. 20:17). This commandment deals with a very subtle, pervasive sin. Edith Schaeffer in her provocative book *Lifelines* points out that this last commandment is one that touches all the others. Covetousness is an internal sin, hard to detect from the outside, but if allowed to grow and fester can lead a person to break all the other commandments. Our desire to possess can lead us to worship material things in place of God, so that we don't love God above all. Nor do we love our neighbor as ourselves if we are jealous of him or her and want for ourselves what our neighbor has. Paul also spoke to the danger of covetousness, or greed. He called it idolatry (Col. 3:5), because when we covet we substitute another god for the true God. He warned Timothy, his son in the Lord, that covetousness and greed are destructive to faith, and James cited coveting as the evil that ignites wrong inner desires and leads to fights, quarrels, and ineffective prayers among Christians:

> People who want to get rich fall into temptation and a trap and into many foolish and harmful desires that plunge men into ruin and destruction. For the love of money is a root of all kinds of evil. Some people, eager for money, have wandered from the faith and pierced themselves with many griefs (1 Tim. 6:9–10).

> What causes fights and quarrels among you? Don't they come from your desires that battle within you? You want something but don't get it. You kill and covet, but you cannot have what you want. You quarrel and fight. You do not have, because you do not ask God. When you ask, you do not receive, because you ask with wrong motives, that you may spend what you get on your pleasures (James 4:1–3).

Jesus longed for the young brother to recognize that wealth and material possessions have no eternal value and are not important compared with the joys that God has for us if we put him first. How opposite is this message from that which bombards us daily from our media. The common theme today is that we only go around life's merry-go-round once, so grab the brass ring now and live it up. The more we buy and possess the happier we will be. Jesus, on the other hand, wanted the young man to see that the inheritance he so much desired for himself would not bring him lasting satisfaction. To drive home his point, he followed his warning with a very insightful story.

## The Parable

> And he told them this parable: "The ground of a certain rich man produced a good crop. He thought to himself,

'What shall I do? I have no place to store my crops.' Then
he said, 'This is what I'll do. I will tear down my barns and
build bigger ones, and there I will store all my grain and my
goods. And I'll say to myself, 'You have plenty of good
things laid up for many years. Take life easy; eat, drink and
be merry." But God said to him, 'You fool! This very night
your life will be demanded from you. Then who will get
what you have prepared for yourself?'" (Luke 12:16–20).

The story's facts about the main character in the story
are simply that he was rich and that his land produced a
bumper crop, apparently much larger than he had anticipated and planned for. Did he earn this large yield through
extra planning and effort that year? Probably not. His crop
was very likely an unearned benefit arising from circumstances beyond his control, such as rain and favorable
weather. In a word, it was a gift from God, but the rich man
did not see it that way. The picture Jesus gave is of a man
rubbing his hands in glee, patting himself on the back, and
setting out to find a way to protect his unexpected bonanza
and keep it all for himself.

### The Problem

His great windfall created a problem for the wealthy
farmer, as often happens. He now began to fret and worry
that he might lose it. "What shall I do?" he asked himself.
"I have no place to store my crops." It didn't seem to occur
to him that he might have had enough goods stashed away
already. If his present barns were crammed full, weren't
there some useful alternatives? He might have given the
unneeded surplus to the poor in his area, or to the temple
in support of the priests. To whom did he go for advice on
his problem? Apparently to no one; he consulted only himself. In his mind, the question was not whether to keep his
bumper crop but how. His actions were those of a selfish
person who lives in a small world defined and bounded on

all sides by himself, with only his own interests in mind. It is not surprising then that such a man came up with a plan consistent with his myopic worldview.

### The Grand Plan

The rich man said, "This is what I'll do. I will tear down my barns and build bigger ones, and there I will store all my grain and my goods. And I'll say to myself, 'You have plenty of good things laid up for many years. Take life easy; eat, drink and be merry.'" Notice all the personal and possessive pronouns—six in verse 18 alone. God's gift of a bumper crop had become "*my* grain and *my* goods." His grand plan was to keep all of it for the benefit of his favorite charity: himself.

The rich man's good fortune allowed him to take early retirement. But when it was time to give a retirement party, who would celebrate with him? His family? His friends? Neighbors who loved him and were grateful for his generosity? Probably none of the above, for none are mentioned in Jesus' story. He would have to celebrate alone. What a contrast to the reactions of the father of the prodigal son (Luke 15:22–25) and of Matthew (Luke 5:27–30), who both put on big feasts and invited many friends to join in their celebrations when they had reasons to rejoice.

The rich man's problem was not his wealth *per se*; rather, it was how he intended to use it. Isn't this a warning for us today? Who are his present-day counterparts? Wouldn't they be those of us who, during their entire lives, close their eyes to the needs around them and make minimum contributions in either time or money to charities, to their churches, or to other ministries, while at the same time they salt away as much as possible in investments and retirement plans and trust these assets to provide many happy, easy years of eating, drinking, and merrymaking? In effect, they trust in their nest eggs rather than in God for their future happiness. Although it is certainly wise to plan systematically for the future, the real question is: What future do we plan for most seriously—our relatively few remaining years on earth or our eternity with God in heaven?

### God's Judgment

Now the story takes a dramatic turn. A second voice breaks in—the voice of Almighty God. "You fool! This very night your life will be demanded from you. Then who will get what you have prepared for yourself?" We don't know how much time passed between verses 19 and 20 of Luke 12. Did God voice this judgment just after the rich man announced his plan, or did he wait until the barns were built, the crops stored, and the rich man was ready to relax and begin to enjoy his retirement? Whatever the timing, God's pronouncement was that, because he had planned for himself alone, he would also die alone. All his goods and grain, selfishly stored only for himself, would now go to others. Everything the rich man possessed—his original riches, his bumper crop, and even his life—were all gifts from God which were on loan to him and subject to recall at any moment. These were facts the rich man failed to consider. He never thought or saw beyond his small material world. In the end, his possessions possessed him; they were all he could think about. But when God summoned him, he had to leave it all behind. He went to bed rich that night, but by morning he had nothing, for he could take nothing of what he owned with him. He had made no spiritual investments for his future.

Jesus' story ended abruptly without recording any more details or any response from the rich man to the voice of God. If we were telling the story, what might we add? Would we have the rich man weep and beg forgiveness? Would we have him repent like Ebenezer Scrooge and quickly try to find and help the Tiny Tims in his neighborhood? Would we add that he died from fright at hearing the voice of God, or that God let him die of a heart attack induced by his rich, fatty diet? It's interesting to imagine various possibilities, but Jesus added nothing. He left us with a brief story that challenges us to consider how we use God's generous gifts to us and if we are ready to have God call back the loan of our lives "this very night." The apostle James gave us a similar warning along with a reminder that our planning should involve the Lord:

> Now listen, you who say, "Today or tomorrow we will go to this or that city, spend a year there, carry on business and make money." Why, you do not even know what will happen tomorrow. What is your life? You are a mist that appears for a little while and then vanishes. Instead, you ought to say, "If it is the Lord's will, we will live and do this or that" (James 4:13–15).

### The Second Warning (Luke 12:21)

Jesus ended his story with God's thundering condemnation. He then added force to the point of his parable with this additional warning: "This is how it will be with anyone who stores up things for himself, but is not rich toward God." We understand very well what it means to store up things for ourselves, but what does it mean to be "rich toward God"? What is it that God expects from us? Whatever else this phrase means, we can conclude from the way Jesus used it in his warning that it is the opposite of selfishly storing up goods for ourselves. Thus, being rich toward God must refer to the *unselfish* use of our material resources for the benefit of others. Perhaps the clearest explanation of what Jesus had in mind by this phrase was his graphic picture of the separation of the sheep and the goats at the final judgment:

> Then the King will say to those on his right, "Come, you who are blessed by my Father; take your inheritance, the kingdom prepared for you since the creation of the world. For I was

hungry and you gave me something to eat, I was thirsty and you gave me something to drink, I was a stranger and you invited me in, I needed clothes and you clothed me, I was sick and you looked after me, I was in prison and you came to visit me." Then the righteous will answer him, "Lord, when did we [do these things]?" The king will reply, "I tell you the truth, whatever you did for one of the least of these brothers of mine, you did for me" (Matt. 25:34–40).

The apostle Paul sounded a similar theme when he wrote to Timothy:

Tell those who are rich not to be proud and not to trust in their money, which will soon be gone, but their pride and trust should be in the living God who always richly gives us all we need for our enjoyment. Tell them to use their money to do good. They should be rich in good works and should give happily to those in need, always being ready to share with others whatever God has given them. By doing this they will be storing up real treasure for themselves in heaven—it is the only safe investment for eternity! (1 Tim. 6:17–19 TLB)

How easy it is for us to get absorbed in acquiring material things or to become deeply involved in activities or organizations that feed our vanity but are of little or no lasting value. What are the things that we do that drain us of all our time, energy, and resources and leave us spiritually poor? Think about your activities and concerns of the past week and draw up your own list. These things we do that compete with our heavenly treasures may not be bad in themselves, but we can become so busy with them that we literally have no time for God, his Word, his people, or helping the least of our brothers.

In many ways, our society seems to be moving headlong down the same path as the rich fool. Based on a survey of what Americans think about money, the Sunday magazine

*Parade* on October 28, 1991, concluded that most Americans believed money to be the key to the good life, and 80 per-cent said that their lives were at least "somewhat controlled" by money. One interviewee held down three jobs so that his wife and two children could have a nice home with a pool in a better part of town. He said, "If you have lots of money, you can buy some happiness." Let's hope that his life isn't demanded from him as a result of a stress–induced heart attack before he gets to enjoy his home and children.

American consumers are going deeper and deeper into debt, often to support their coveted lifestyles and to "keep up with the Joneses." Forty per cent of the families inter-viewed by *Parade* admitted to having problems paying their debts. We Americans seem to be determined to build big-ger barns, only we have added a new wrinkle. We borrow the money to build the barns and then use credit cards to buy things to fill them. And we Christians have a strong tendency to go right along with the crowd. We are not immune from wanting what our neighbors have. But when we do this, we find out the hard way that financial worries and concerns make it difficult to put God first. It is only as we seek to involve God in planning the uses of our resources of time, abilities, and possessions and ask him to help us give him his proper place in our lives that he will send his Spirit to help us do this and to be rich toward God.

Too often we Christians assume that material posses-sions are included among the blessings God desires for his children and forget the temptations and pitfalls they pre-sent. A popular theme of some pastors and television evan-gelists during the booming decade of the 1980s was a gospel of prosperity—that Christians have a right to expect good health, happiness, and prosperity. This, they insisted, was the evidence of God's love and blessing upon his people. If we would just trust God, we could expect good health and our lives would be worry free, successful, and beauti-ful. One former proponent of this message was Jim Bakker, now serving an eighteen-year prison sentence after being convicted on twenty-four counts of fraud. Bakker has reevaluated his position while in prison. In a recent letter to his friends he wrote the following:

> Many today believe that the evidence of God's blessing on them is a new car, a house, a good job, and riches. . . . That is far from the truth of God's Word. . . . Jesus did not teach riches were a sign of God's blessing. . . . I have spent months reading every word Jesus spoke. I wrote them out over and over, and I read them over and over again. There is no way, if you take the whole counsel of God's Word, that you can equate riches or material things as a sign of God's blessing.

> I have asked God to forgive me and I ask all who have sat under my ministry to forgive me for preaching a gospel emphasizing earthly prosperity. If we equate earthly possessions and earthly relationships with God's favor, what are we going to tell the billions of those living in poverty?

> Jesus said, "Narrow is the way that leads to life and few there be that find it." It's time the call from the pulpit be changed from "Who wants the life of pleasure and good things?" to "Who will come forward to accept Jesus Christ and the fellowship of his suffering?"

> Serving Christ today to many is a wonderful and entertaining musical program, and the preaching of earthly benefit. . . . I believe God is grieved when we cannot delay self-gratification for earthly things in exchange for life in eternity with him.

These are powerful words from this repentant evangelist— a man from whom God recalled, almost overnight, his status, honor, and possessions. They force us to recall Jesus' message in this parable and in his warnings to the young brother, to think about what is really important in life. God wants the best for his children: that we are well fed and well dressed, but with spiritual, imperishable food and clothing. He feeds and sustains us with the living bread of his Word, and he promises to clothe us with the righteousness of Christ. These are the true riches—gifts which dwarf to insignificance our temporal possessions that now seem so important.

Being showered with spiritual blessings is part of the glorious inheritance God promises when we are adopted as his children through faith in Christ. Paul wrote, "If you belong to Christ, then you are Abraham's seed, and heirs according to the promise" (Gal. 3:29). He also wrote: "The Spirit himself testifies with our spirit that we are God's children. Now if we are children, then we are heirs—heirs of God and co-heirs with Christ" (Rom. 8:16–17). What an inheritance—to have Christ's presence with us now and to share Christ's glory for all eternity! This is the inheritance of supreme value that the preoccupied young man in Jesus' audience was in danger of missing. He was so consumed with worry about the paltry sum he thought his brother was withholding from him that he couldn't listen to the words of life from the lips of Jesus. Perhaps Jesus' parable woke him up to realize that his treasure and his heart were bound up with the temporal instead of the eternal. May Jesus' words also burn into our hearts his perspective on what is important in life and ignite within us an attitude of love, joy, and hope because we share in his glorious inheritance, for

> No eye has seen,
>     no ear has heard,
> no mind has conceived
>     what God has prepared for those
>     who love him (1 Cor. 2:9).

# Suggestions for Group Leaders

1. Keep in mind that the purpose of group discussion is to help all the members understand the Bible, implement the truths learned, refresh each other by exchanging thoughts, impressions, and ideas, and to support the formation of bonds of friendship.

2. Encourage the members to set aside a daily time for study and prayer.

3. Remind the members to write out answers. Expressing oneself on paper clarifies thoughts and analyzes understanding. Because written answers are succinct and thoughtful, discussion will be enlivened.

4. Be familiar enough with the lesson so you can identify questions that can most easily be omitted if time is short. Select and adapt an appropriate number of questions so that the lesson topic can be completed. Reword the question if the group feels it is unclear. Covering too little material is discouraging to the

class. Skip the questions that cover material the class has already discussed. Often the last questions are the most thought-provoking. Choose questions that create lively and profitable interchange of views.

5. Encourage all members to participate. Often the less vocal people have amazingly thoughtful contributions.

6. Keep the group focused on the passage studied, emphasizing that answers should come from Scripture. Steer the discussion away from tangents. Sidestep controversial subjects, Christian causes, political action, and so forth. Ask, "Where did you find that in this passage?" "Did anyone find a thought not yet mentioned?"

7. Pick up on any "live news" of spiritual growth, recent actions taken, honest admissions of inadequacy or failures, and desire for prayer. Be sensitive to "beginners" in the Christian walk, recognizing their need to share new discoveries, joys, commitments, and decisions.

8. Spend time in prayer as you prepare for the lesson. Remember to pray for each member. Pray daily for yourself to have a listening ear, a sensitive heart, and

an effervescent and contagious spirit of joy as you lead. Pray you will affirm each member who contributes. Ask God to give you a variety of ways to do this.

## Closing Remarks

Prepared closing remarks are valuable (and essential) for clearing up misunderstandings of the passage, for further teachings, for applying the Scripture to current situations, and for challenging each individual to action. Before the meeting decide on how much time to allow for discussion and closing remarks, and follow the timetable.